The Truth about College Admission Workbook

The Truth about
COLLEGE
ADMISSION
WORKBOOK

· ·

A FAMILY ORGANIZER
FOR YOUR COLLEGE SEARCH

· ·

Brennan Barnard
and Rick Clark

JOHNS HOPKINS UNIVERSITY PRESS

Baltimore

© 2021 Johns Hopkins University Press
All rights reserved. Published 2021
Printed in the United States of America on acid-free paper
9 8 7 6 5 4 3 2

Johns Hopkins University Press
2715 North Charles Street
Baltimore, Maryland 21218
www.press.jhu.edu

Library of Congress Cataloging-in-Publication Data

Names: Barnard, Brennan E., 1974– author. | Clark, Rick, 1974– author.
Title: The truth about college admission : a family guide to getting in and staying together /
    Brennan Barnard and Rick Clark.
Description: Second edition. | Baltimore : Johns Hopkins University Press, [2023] | Includes
    bibliographical references and index.
Identifiers: LCCN 2022061228 | ISBN 9781421447483 (paperback) | ISBN 9781421447490 (ebook)
Subjects: LCSH: Universities and colleges—United States—Admission. | College choice—
    United States.
Classification: LCC LB2351.2 .B37 2023 | DDC 378.1/610973—dc23/eng/20221221
LC record available at https://lccn.loc.gov/2022061228

A catalog record for this book is available from the British Library.

Illustration Credits: **xv** HuHu Lin, Adobe Stock; **xv** From "Why Experience Gifts Are Better
Than Material Things," HostelWorld, November 30, 2018, https://www.hostelworld.com/blog
/experience-gifts-better-than-material-things/; **82** Adapted from Georgia Institute of Technology
Undergraduate Admission, *College Selection Guide*, 2019, https://admission.gatech.edu/sites/default
/files/images/searchpiece/college_guide.pdf; **207** Vandhira, Adobe Stock; **243** Reprinted with
the permission of Adam Zyglis.

*Special discounts are available for bulk purchases of this book. For more information, please contact Special
Sales at specialsales@jh.edu.*

For our children, AJ, Elizabeth, Rebecca, and Samuel
We love you and we are proud of you!

Contents

PART I

PART II

Chapter 4. Creating a College List   **72**

Chapter 5. The College Visit   **107**

PART III

Chapter 6. Admission Factors I: What Are Colleges Looking for Academically?   126

Chapter 7. Admission Factors II: What Are Colleges Looking for outside the Classroom?   147

PART IV

How to Use This Workbook

Students, we created this workbook as a resource for you. We know you are smart, motivated, and willing to put in the thought and time necessary to ensure your admission experience is not a passive one but rather an opportunity to reflect, stretch, grow, and learn.

In this hands-on guide, our goal is to help you engage fully and meaningfully in your college search, application, and decision and to assist you in proactively initiating important conversations with your family along the way.

Ideally you will take advantage of every exercise in this guide, but it is also designed to allow individuals, families, and schools to select those activities most helpful and applicable to a student's unique experience. Our hope is that you will adapt these resources and share them, in order to lead a less transactional and more intentional and educational experience of searching for and applying to college.

Each chapter mirrors those in our book *The Truth about College Admission: A Family Guide to Getting In and Staying Together*. While we suggest reading the book first as context, this workbook was developed to stand alone as well. Here, each chapter begins with a brief overview of a topic and offers some general thoughts to help you frame your approach to the exercises. What follows is a series of sections with exercises that you, the student, are meant to complete. Any section fronted by the word *family*, such as "Family Forward," addresses your parents or other family members who are involved in your admission experience. These sections have exercises for your family members to complete that are identical or similar to your exercises. And sections titled "Come Together," which appear at or near the end of chapters, are meant for you and your family members to read together. In these, we invite you and your family members to share what you have all learned and discuss how it applies to your college search. The one exception to this pattern is chapter 3, the whole of which student and family are meant to read together.

Our hope is that you will write down your responses to questions and fill in forms as completely as possible. As you move through the admission experience, it will be helpful to refer back to your exercises and trace the evolution of your search.

Authors' Note: As educators and admission professionals, we believe strongly in the power of higher education to transform lives and benefit both the individual and society, but we also acknowledge that the path to college is not for everyone. This workbook is written for students and families who have decided that pursuing a college degree is both valuable and important. Our intention is to provide a guide for those navigating college admission that is more healthy, broad, and unified than we commonly see. We use the words *family* and *parents* as catchall terms to simplify the flow of our recommendations. We are aware, however, that families come in all shapes and sizes and that "parents" could include guardians, grandparents, or other trusted adults who are supporting young people through this experience. We want to honor the power of family as representing connection and community in helping students both dream and plan for their future. Although we focus our recommendations on traditional college-age students, we hope this workbook will serve as a valuable resource and important conversation tool for anyone engaging in the college search and application journey.

Introduction

At a conference in Newport, Rhode Island, a few summers ago, I (Rick) entered my name in a raffle to take a helicopter tour. On the day of the drawing, the organizer announced her 2-year-old son would be selecting the three lucky winners. I almost stood up instantly because I knew one of the spots was mine. I'm not sure what it is exactly, but me and 2-year-olds . . . we get each other. And sure enough, my name was the first one called.

A helicopter tour is completely different from a plane ride. When you board a plane, you are almost singularly focused on *where* you are going. Destination is king. Delays, reroutes, snoring passengers, lack of coffee, and turbulence are frustrating, annoying, scary, or some combination of all of these (looking at you, flight 225). Unfortunately, that is the same approach many students take when they search for and apply to colleges. They want to know what the rules are, how to avoid the pitfalls, and the smoothest path to a specific campus.

In contrast, a helicopter tour is not about getting somewhere in particular, because you end up landing in the same spot you started from. Instead, it is about adjusting your vantage point, exploring, appreciating, changing your perspective, and enjoying the experience with the people alongside you. That is what this workbook is all about. Our goal is to help you *tour* with vision and confidence versus *flying through* anxiously. Ultimately, the exercises and activities that follow are more about how you arrive on a college campus than precisely where you land.

Try this

Before we go any further, let's play a quick word association game. (*Do not skip this or skim down the page.*) Write down or think quickly about the first three to five words or phrases that come to mind when you read or hear the word **college**.

1.

2.

3.

4.

5.

Having asked this question around the country in various cities and communities, particularly when parents are in the room, the responses are usually extremely hopeful and life-affirming. We see a lot of smiles and hear answers such as *friends, fun, travel, sports,* and *studying,* because ultimately college is exciting! College is an adventure. College is filled with opportunities.

Now write down or think quickly about the first three to five words or phrases that come to mind when you read or hear the words **college admission**.

1.

2.

3.

4.

5.

Boo! Who popped the balloon? How can adding one word steal the hope and joy and excitement of college? Answer: it shouldn't. It does not have to be that way. And there are a few easy ways to prevent that from happening to you.

Change One Word

Traditionally, when journalists and college reps talk about admission, they describe it as a process. We want to push back on that word. Take a minute to search Google Images for the word *process.* (Yes. We seriously want you to take out your phone and do this.)

So what did you find? Probably a lot of flow charts, cogs grinding together, and mechanical, sterile, linear graphics. Notice that almost none of them includes other people.

If you think of all of this as a *process,* then you begin to believe there is one specific and right way to go about it. Your mindset becomes binary. *Process* restricts you to a narrow path that you must follow in order to avoid peril.

Process dictates that one piece must fit perfectly and flow precisely from one thing to the next. And then life happens. You earn a B+ instead of an A in that history class sophomore year, you don't get elected president of the French Club, you tear your ACL and can't play soccer as a junior, the mission trip gets canceled, and they pick Derek over you for the last slot as a translation volunteer at the hospital.

If this is a process, then you absolutely should—or should not—"do this the way your older sister did." Process is filled with don'ts. Process is a tight-rope. Process means if you miss a certain ingredient, the recipe is a bust. Everything is ruined.

Now take a minute to search Google Images for *experiences*. What do you find and how does it compare to *process*?

Experiences should help you breathe. These images are more open, more fluid, and more relational. In these pictures you find people looking out over high places considering their options. They have vision, perspective, and freedom. *Experience* images are filled with boats in the water or bikes on the trail. There is variety and a wide lens. *Experiences* facilitate relationships, inspire dreams, and account for a breadth of decisions, routes, and ultimate results or destinations.

For some reason, people tend to think of the college attendance experience and the college admission experience as separate entities. The truth is the two are closely linked. They are both about developing critical thinking skills, seeing a bigger picture, seeking diverse voices, researching information, being comfortable with some gray areas and unknowns, weighing options, self-discovery, questioning data, understanding historical context, and keeping a broad (ideally global) perspective.

In this workbook, our goal is to provide you with activities and exercises designed to enrich your experience of searching for, applying to, choosing, and ultimately thriving at a college that is a good match for your interests, values, and dreams. If *stress*, *tests*, *control*, and *pressure* creep in too much, it is a good sign you are trying to *fly* again and need to recalibrate and regain perspective.

Again, helicopters not airplanes, friends. Strap in and let's get started!

Playlist

In *The Truth about College Admission*, we started each chapter with song lyrics that went along with the chapter's central idea.

Chapter 1: "We thought we had all the answers. It was the questions we had wrong." — "11 O'Clock Tick Tock" by U2

Chapter 2: "And the people in the houses / All went to the university, / Where they were put in boxes / And they came out all the same." — "Little Boxes" by Walk Off the Earth

Chapter 3: "Let's stay together / Lovin' you whether / Times are good or bad, happy or sad." — "Let's Stay Together" by Al Green

Chapter 4: "I really want to know (Who are you?) / Tell me who are you?" — "Who are You" by The Who

Chapter 5: "I hope you never fear those mountains in the distance / Never settle for the path of least resistance / Livin' might mean takin' chances, but they're worth takin'." — "I Hope You Dance" by Lee Ann Womack

Chapter 6: "Gonna cruise out of this city / Head down to the sea / Gonna shout out at the ocean / Hey it's me / And I feel like a number." — "Feel Like a Number" by Bob Seger

Chapter 7: "It's a little bit of everything, / It's the matador and the bull / It's the suggested daily dosage / It's the red moon when it's full. / All these psychics and these doctors / They're alright and they're all wrong, / It's like trying to make out every word / When they should simply hum along. / It's not some message written in the dark / Or some truth that no one's seen. / It's a little bit of everything." — "A Little Bit of Everything" by Dawes

Chapter 8: "Why do we never get an answer / When we are knocking at the door / Because the truth is hard to swallow / That's what the war of love is for." — "Question" by The Moody Blues

Chapter 9: "Burn the ships, cut the ties / Send a flare into the night / Say a prayer, turn the tide." — "Burn the Ships" by King and Country

Chapter 10: "Get up everybody and sing / Everyone can see we're together / As we walk on by / And we fly just like birds of a feather." — "We Are Family" by Sister Sledge

As you go through this workbook, we hope you will think about songs that come to mind as you are reading, learning, and considering your college options. Whether they be themed by chapter or just a song that pops into your head, make your own family or individual college admission playlist. This will be helpful to play when you are writing essays, traveling to visit a campus, or sitting down to make your final college choice.

We'd love to know the songs you add, so let us know on Twitter.

Rick Clark, @clark2college
Brennan Barnard, @BarnardBrennan

Part I

Chapter 1

Why Are You Going to College?

High school should be a time not only to learn and grow but also to question, explore, challenge, and reflect. Unfortunately, too often, in an effort to achieve and succeed, students feel like they are on a treadmill or a balance beam, where pausing to genuinely consider motivations and aspirations or taking risks is not an option. Too many students miss this, but your college admission experience is an invitation to slow down, take a breath, dial things back, and start with simple but incredibly important questions.

As a student thinking about college, you have lots of questions and concerns that inevitably create some doubt: How do I do this? Where should I look? What should I be doing? Will any school admit me? When do I begin? Can I be successful? Which school will be right? Your parents and other family members have their own set of questions: How do we best support our students? What is our role in the search and application experience? How hands-on should we be? What timeline should we follow? What are we missing? How do we pay for this? Trust us. We'll get there in this workbook. But for now, we want you to focus on one principal foundational question: *Why do you want to go to college?*

Spoiler alert: There is no one right answer. The answer for *you* by definition should be unique. It is going to take some work, some time, and most of all a willingness to be honest with yourself. None of that is easy, but we are confident you will begin to see how important and fun it can be to discover your truth.

Our goal in this chapter is to provide resources and exercises to guide and encourage you. We also provide you with reflections to help you begin to articulate what is important to you, what you value, what your hopes are, what your unique strengths are, and what type of experience you are looking for in college. This is not a static or linear exercise, so expect your answers to change along the way as you learn and are exposed to more of the college search. Sometimes answering questions and working through these activities will lead to more questions. That is a good thing. Refining and modifying means you are engaged, learning, and open—all qualities that will serve you well in your actual college experience too.

We are confident that if you set a firm foundation, embrace a dynamic mindset, and clarify your approach and answers to the most simple but critical questions, you will not only thrive in your college search and selection experience but also be able to communicate openly and honestly with your family along the way.

1.1
The Cornerstone Question: *Why?*

Do you want to go to college?

☐ Yes

☐ No

☐ Maybe

Why?

Please list YOUR three top reasons for wanting to attend college and earn a higher degree:

•

•

•

Please share reasons that OTHER PEOPLE in your life might want you to go to college:

•

•

We know this may sound extremely basic, but, trust us, you have to crawl before you walk. Too few students are willing and intentional enough to ask fundamental questions. Ultimately, you will be able to come back to these answers and use them as the filter through which you consider the colleges you want to research, visit, apply to, and ultimately select to attend.

1.2

Student Self-Reflection

You know yourself better than anyone. Unfortunately, despite the inordinate amount of time we spend in our own heads, we often fail to collect our thoughts in intentional, organized ways. The following questions invite you to do just that. There are a lot here, and at the very least you should read and consider them all. Write your answers down or type them out (or voice-record them on your phone) for three to five questions from each section below. This will help you begin to frame your college search around who you are and what you value. This exercise will also be helpful when you are preparing for scholarship or admission interviews and brainstorming essay or short-answers responses.

You

What brings you joy?

What makes you the most afraid?

What values are most important to you?

What do you care about the most?

If you could live the last ten years again, what if anything would you do differently?

What concerns you the most?

Which adjectives would you use to describe yourself?

If you had to create a bumper sticker that best spoke to your identity, what would it say and why?

Describe a time or moment when you felt at your best.

What are you grateful for?

What do you wish was different?

What has changed about you?

When have you felt conflicted?

What do you need?

How important are approval and recognition to you?

How do you respond to pressure, competition, or challenge?

How do you react to failure, disappointment, or criticism?

What are your finest qualities?

What are your weaknesses?

How have you grown or changed during your high school years?

How will you describe yourself to your future college roommate?

Your environment and family

Describe your family.

Describe your community.

What is your role in your family (for example, peacemaker, comic relief, planner)?

How has your environment shaped you and your interests?

What would you change about your community?

What is the most controversial issue being discussed in your school or community? (How does the issue concern you? What has been your reaction to the controversy? What is your opinion?)

What circumstances or experiences have shaped your growth and way of thinking?

Your people

Describe the individuals whom you consider to be your best friends, critics, and advocates. (For instance, if you were to go on a cross-country road trip, whom would you want with you?)

Who challenges you?

What is your role in your group of friends?

Whom do you hope to be surrounded by in college?

Who holds you to high standards?

What support do you seek from friends?

What frustrates you most about people?

Whom do you hope you will meet, connect with, and learn from in college?

Do you often encounter people who think or act differently than you?

What viewpoints challenge you the most? How do you respond? From these experiences, what have you learned about yourself and others?

How would someone who knows you well describe you? Would you agree with their assessment?

How would you describe the perfect roommate for you?

Which relationships are most important to you and why?

How are you influenced by others who are important to you?

What pressures have you felt to conform?

Your learning

What about your high school do you appreciate most?

What would you change about your high school?

Which classes do you look forward to the most? Why?

Which classes have been the most challenging? Why?

Describe your favorite teacher. What makes that teacher influential or effective?

How do you learn best?

What is your ideal classroom environment?

What do you like to learn about outside class?

How well prepared do you feel for college?

What would you miss most if you could not go to school?

What would you eliminate from your school day?

What books or textbooks from your courses have you enjoyed most?

What do you read outside class?

Which websites do you visit most often?

Which podcasts do you listen to?

What YouTube channels, Instagram feeds, etc., do you follow?

If you read newspapers or digital publications, which do you regularly read and what stories do you prefer to explore?

What are your academic interests?

What do you choose to learn when you can learn on your own? (Consider interests pursued apart from class assignments, such as topics chosen for research projects, lab reports, independent projects, independent reading, school activities, and jobs or volunteer work.)

What do your choices show about your interests and the way you like to learn?

How much do you genuinely like to read, discuss issues, and exchange ideas?

What has been your most stimulating intellectual experience?

In what areas of skill or knowledge do you feel confident? In what areas do you feel inadequately prepared for college study?

Have you lived up to your potential in high school?

Is your academic record an accurate measure of your ability and potential? (If not, why?)

Do you think that your SAT or ACT scores are an accurate measure of your ability and potential? (If not, why?)

Are there any outside circumstances in your recent experience or background that have interfered with your academic achievement? (Think of factors over which you have control and those things that are outside your control at school and at home.)

Your interests and involvement

What movies do you enjoy?

What music do you listen to?

If you had a day to do anything, how would you spend it?

What activity are you involved in that fulfills you?

What do you wish you could do more of?

What would you like to do less of?

What have you always wanted to try?

Of your interests and strengths, which would you most like to develop?

Which activities have meant the most to you?

Which of your activities show a pattern of commitment, competence, and/or contribution? (How so?)

How have your interests been encouraged or limited by your school and home?

Your future

As a younger child, what if anything did you want to be when you grew up?

Is there anything you have ever secretly wanted to be?

What kind of person would you like to become?

If you had six to twelve months to go anywhere and do anything you wanted, where would you go and what would you do?

What opportunities do you want the college experience to provide in the future?

Why are you willing to work hard academically beyond high school to earn a college degree?

What is most important to you as you leave high school and look ahead at your next chapter?

What are some of the potential fields of study (majors, minors, areas of interest) and career options you think about?

Are you considering graduate or professional school?

What do you think it means to live a good life?

What obstacles do you face, if any, in living a good life?

What does success mean to you?

What is a problem that you want to solve?

Admission readers will frequently tell you, "We just want to hear your voice." Self-awareness is where that all begins. While we know that these questions are a lot to consider and work through, your answers will be invaluable as you move forward. (Some of these questions were inspired by long-time college admission professional Susan Tree, former director of college counseling at Westtown School and admission officer at Bates College.)

1.3

Exploring Why

You may have talked about college with family and friends, but often these conversations are somewhat superficial. This exercise encourages you to have intentional discussions with at least two people about college. Perhaps choose a family member, a current college student or recent college graduate, employer, teacher, coach, or friend's parent. Use these prompts to help you gain meaningful feedback.

Questions you might want to ask

- Why did you go to college?
- Where did you go to college?
- Where else did you consider going or apply to?
- How would you go about searching for and applying to college differently today?
- If you had it to do over, how would you go about your college experience differently?
- What experiences are most memorable from your search or selection journey?
- What are the biggest mistakes you believe you made?
- What surprised you or what do you wish you had known earlier?
- What did you do right?
- What else should I be asking about college?

Again, *why?* is your cornerstone question. Use it that way. When you receive information from colleges in the mail, when someone suggests you apply to a specific college, when friends or classmates are "all" going to a certain school, run it through your *why* filter.

Answers

- Interviewee #1 Name: _____

  College Attended: _____

What did you learn from your conversation with this individual?

What surprised you?

Does this change how you approach your college search? If so, how?

- Interviewee #2 Name: _____

  College Attended: _____

What did you learn from your conversation with this individual?

What surprised you?

Does this change how you approach your college search? If so, how?

1.4

Family Forward

I (Brennan) was a stay-at-home father for the first three years of my children's lives. These were some of the best—and most challenging—years of my adult life. It was around the time that I returned to work that my kids began the incessant questioning of "why?" Coincidence? I think not! While as parents we are excited to see our kids' growing curiosity about the world around them, the "why?" refrain can wear us down. Especially when, in our perpetually sleep-deprived existence, we lack a coherent answer to their inquiries. We often find ourselves making up responses. "Why is a Cheerio round?" ". . . Umm, because it fits more uniformly into a toddler's nose that way?"

As they grow older and enter school, students are inundated with answers to questions they might not even know they have. Information is fed to them in a steady stream, just as adults often experience in their busy work and daily lives. Especially in the age of digital technology and instant access to answers, it is easy to stop asking the big question of "why?" In many ways, students' lives—and those of their parents—seem scripted, and we go through the motions.

The reality is that we parents still don't know the answer to our children's "why?" any more than we did with the Cheerio. We can, however, return the favor and ask them why. We can encourage them to reflect on what they value and hope for and to consider the experiences they want to have as they journey forward. The exercises in this chapter asked students to do just that, and now parents have their turn to answer similar questions. Then we will invite parents and children to come together to share your responses and consider next steps. This will set the stage for the whole college search and application experience, so do not take shortcuts or try to surge ahead without first having these critical conversations.

1.5

Family Cornerstone

Do you want your child to attend college?

☐ Yes

☐ No

☐ Maybe

Why?

Please list your top three reasons for wanting your child to attend college and earn a higher degree (elaborate as much as possible).

Why not? / maybe?

Please list any doubts you have or reasons that you feel college might not be right for your child.

In the Come Together activity of this chapter, we will be asking parents to share their answers with their student. We have found that many parents think they have already said these things to their kids. Taking the time to articulate your answers to this cornerstone question is a pivotal first step toward building trust and getting on the same page as a family.

1.6

Family Reflection

You know your child better than anyone. The following questions invite you to reflect, first on you, your family, and community, and then on what you know about your child. Choose three to five questions in each section, and write down your answers without thinking about them. This, along with your child's answers to similar questions, will help you begin to frame the college search around who they are and what they value.

You

What makes you the most afraid?

What do you care about most?

What concerns you the most?

Which adjectives would you use to describe yourself?

What are you grateful for?

What do you wish were different?

When have you felt conflicted?

What brings you joy?

Your environment and family

Describe your family.

Describe your community.

What is your child's role in your family (e.g., peacemaker, comic relief, planner)?

How has your environment shaped your child and their interests?

What values are most important to your family?

How do the opinions of others in your community impact you?

How do the opinions of others in your community impact your child?

Your child

If you had to create a bumper sticker that best spoke to your child's identity, what would it say and why?

What brings your child joy?

What makes your child the most afraid?

What values are most important to your child?

What does your child care about most?

What concerns your child the most?

Which adjectives would you use to describe your child?

When has your child felt conflicted?

What does your child need to thrive?

How important are approval and recognition to your child?

How does your child respond to pressure, competition, or challenge?

How does your child react to failure, disappointment, or criticism?

What are your child's finest qualities?

What are your child's weaknesses?

How has your child grown or changed during their high school years?

Your child's friends

Describe your child's closest friends.

What is your child's role in their friend group?

Who are the kinds of people you hope your child will meet, connect with, and learn from in college?

Your child's learning

What have you appreciated most about your child's education?

What would you change about your child's educational experiences?

How does your child learn best?

What does your child like to learn about outside class?

How well prepared do you think your child is for college?

What school books or textbooks has your child enjoyed most?

What do they read outside class?

Your child's interests and involvement

What movies does your child enjoy?

What music does your child listen to?

Of your child's interests and strengths, which do you wish they would develop more?

Your child's future

As a younger child, what if anything did they want to be when they grew up?

What expectations do you have for your child's future?

What opportunities do you want the college experience to provide for your child in the future?

Why would you invest a lot of money in a college education?

How much can you, and should you, pay for this opportunity?

Our hope is that these prompts help you focus not on *where* your child "should go to college" but instead on *who* they really are as a person and a student. Taking the time to consider, record, and regularly revisit your answers in this activity will enable you to be an invaluable resource and support as your family begins and travels through the college admission experience.

1.7

Come Together

We have asked you all to consider a *lot* of questions in this chapter. Probably more self-reflection then you have done in a while. Take a deep breath (and remember to do this often). Now it is time to articulate to one another what you have identified. This will be good practice for students as they imagine how they will communicate with colleges about who they are and what they want.

"Why" wrap-up

Students: You get to start.

Share your top three reasons for wanting to go to college—your "why." Be as specific as possible and elaborate on your answers.

Explain why you think others in your life want you to go to college.

What did you learn about the experiences of those you interviewed and why they went to college?

Parents: Were you surprised by any of your student's reasons for wanting to go to college? Were their impressions of your hopes accurate? Okay, now it is your turn.

Share why you think your student should or should not go to college.

What doubts do you have, if any?

Reflection review

Students: Your self-reflection exercise was divided into six sections. Pick one or two of your answers from questions in each of the sections and share them with your family. Pick responses that maybe surprised you or stumped you at first.

- You
- Your Environment and Family
- Your People
- Your Learning
- Your Interests and Involvement
- Your Future

Parents: You knew this was coming. Time for you to share some of your responses to questions about you and your student.

- You
- Your Environment and Family
- Your Child
- Your Child's Friends
- Your Child's Learning

- Your Child's Interests and Involvement

- Your Child's Future

Discuss your reflections together.

What surprised you about each other's responses?

What did you answer similarly?

Where did you not agree?

What has been left unsaid?

Final Thoughts

Spend some time as a family talking about what all of the introspection you have done, and discussion you have had, as individuals and together means for starting the college search. The questions you have explored will be helpful to revisit throughout this journey and to return to often to keep your internal compass pointing in the right direction and to ground your experience.

Chapter 2

Remapping the Admission Landscape

I (Rick) have traveled extensively throughout the United States and overseas. At last count, forty-five states and five continents. Beyond that, I have always loved looking at maps, studying American history, and can generally hold my own at Tuesday Night Trivia when geography questions come up.

However, a few years ago I visited Minnesota for the first time. After flying in late at night, I put on my running shoes early the next morning to explore the city of Minneapolis before the day got rolling. At the hotel's front desk, I asked for a recommendation of a good route to get a sense of the area. "Oh. Of course. I'd recommend the Bridge Run. It's about six miles long and crosses the river four times. I think you'll love it."

I pray the hotel did not have a camera on the front desk that morning to capture the next part of our exchange.

"Oh, great. What river is it?" Honestly, I thought she was going to rattle off some obscure name that I may have heard mentioned or seen once or twice on a map.

She paused, and I noticed her eyebrows raise slightly as she breathed in deeply. And then, with a slight bit of pity in her voice, she said slowly . . . "the Mississippi."

Now, I am pretty sure I held it together in the moment, but it was all I could do to bottle up the simultaneous combination of embarrassment and shock that ran through me. "Perfect," I stammered and headed quickly for the door.

Arguably our nation's most famous of rivers, the Mississippi is one I've crossed many times and even swam in once—granted that had happened hundreds of miles south. How could I not realize Minnesota is the state where it starts?

The run across the bridges at sunrise that day was absolutely breathtaking. By the third crossing I had transitioned from being flummoxed and embarrassed to laughing about it. I texted my wife (who lived in Minnesota for five years) a picture from the middle of one of the bridges: "Mississippi River runs through Minneapolis . . . who knew?!" Five minutes later she replied, "Everyone but you, apparently." Ouch. Insult to injury.

I am guessing you can think of a similar situation or revelation—something you read, heard, or learned that changed your view, challenged your assumptions, or expanded your understanding of someone or something. (If you can't, start reading more and hanging around different people.)

In many ways, my experience in Minnesota is illustrative of the limited and misinformed perspective most people have on both college and college admission. They have some exposure but lack the full picture. They rely on personal experience and are so heavily influenced by social media, or what they hear and observe in their small social circle, that their view is understandably narrow—a condition, whether it be in politics, public health, or another issue in society, that inevitably leads to poor decision-making and unnecessary anxiety.

Like college itself, the college admission experience is all about learning, expanding, researching, and being open to new ideas and possibilities. That takes paying attention, reflection, intention, and sometimes tension. This chapter is about helping you see a bigger, more accurate landscape of higher education, broadening your understanding of the amazing choices and options you have, and helping you navigate a path through your college admission experience with a new and more accurate "map."

Enjoy the journey!

2.1

Escape Your Echo Chamber

Write down the names of the first seven colleges or universities that pop into your head.

1.

2.

3.

4.

5.

6.

7.

Now circle the schools that are in your home state; the colleges that a parent, sibling, or other family member attended; the schools that are nationally known in your favorite sport; and any that rhyme with Stanvard.

Are more than 50 percent circled? Congratulations! You are using the right book and, like most people, have the opportunity to see a bigger picture of the higher education landscape in America. One reason that students and their families have anxiety around college admission is because they have a limited, inaccurate, or incomplete understanding of their choices and options. As we discussed in our book, one of our country's biggest strengths is the diversity in our higher education system. The exercises in this chapter are designed to help you see that more fully.

2.2

Run the Numbers

Chapter 1 asked you to consider some big questions. Who am I? What are my hopes, goals, and dreams? And most importantly, answer honestly your cornerstone question: *Why do I want to go to college?* These are critical questions to wrestle with, and we hope you'll continue to reflect on and revisit your answers as you go through this workbook. Ultimately, we hope your focus and energy is already shifting away from exactly *where* you will end up going to college and toward *how* you will arrive there—self-aware, confident, and excited about *your* new community.

The good news is that you have lots of options. Define *lots*. For instance, did you know there are over 4,600 colleges and universities in the United States (including private, public, community colleges, two-year schools, four-year universities, technical, comprehensive, etc.)?

Even if you have determined you want to attend a four-year college or university, you still have about 3,000 choices. Choices, ultimately, are what your college search and selection should be all about. Whether it be researching schools, visiting campuses, applying to a range of institutions, or making a final choice, your goal is to be able to select along the way.

Let's see if we can broaden your view even more.

In the list below, draw a line from the figure in the left column to its match in the right column.

~270	Number of schools included in *Colleges That Change Lives*
~64 percent	Average admit rate of Big 10 universities
~980	Number of American colleges with undergraduate populations under 1,000
~100	Number of American colleges starting with the letter *B*
~55 percent	Number of colleges admitting less than 33 percent of applicants
~300	Number of American universities with undergraduate populations of more than 20,000
~40	Number of public community colleges
~1,500	Average admit rate for four-year colleges

How did you do? Check the answers at the end of this section and see.

The truth is that getting into most colleges and universities around the United States is not the real challenge. There are, in fact, hundreds of academically excellent universities looking to admit and enroll talented students who will not only succeed inside the classroom but also contribute in a meaningful and impactful way to the campus community.

In his book *Demographics and the Demand for Higher Education*, Professor Nathan Grawe cites the precipitous decline in the birth rate resulting from the 2008 economic downturn and predicts its significant impact on the college-going population starting around 2026. Admission deans and directors around the United States were all preparing their administrations for this so-called demographic cliff with its decrease in high school graduates. COVID-19, however, was effectively a huge flood that drastically eroded the cliff. National Clearinghouse data from December 2020 showed US undergraduate enrollment down 4 percent and first-year student enrollment down 16.1 percent compared with 2019. Even more disturbing is that community colleges saw a 22.7 percent dip in enrollment.

Bottom line: If you follow the guidance in this workbook and apply to a "balanced list" of colleges (which we'll address in chapter 4), you are going to be admitted to several great schools from which you can choose. So, if you have not already, take a deep breath . . . and exhale.

Answers

Number of schools included in *Colleges That Change Lives* = ~40

Average admit rate of Big 10 universities = ~55 percent

Number of American colleges with undergraduate populations under 1,000 = ~1,500

Number of American colleges starting with the letter *B* = ~300

Number of colleges admitting less than 33 percent of applicants = ~100

American universities with undergraduate populations over 20,000 = ~270

Number of public community colleges = ~980

Average admit rate for four-year colleges = ~64 percent

We hope you find this information deeply encouraging.

Take a moment to write down one or two stats that surprised you.

Go online and search for the number of colleges and universities in your home state. Are there any you have not heard of before? If so, how many?

What other numbers does this information make you want to investigate?

2.3

Reading Is FUNdamental

Let's take a look at a few passages that reinforce the value and logic of keeping an open mind about the diverse range of colleges to consider. In his book *Where You Go Is Not Who You'll Be*, Frank Bruni provides numerous anecdotes and data that support the wide landscape of college options:

> The chief executive of Wal-Mart, Doug McMillon, went on from the University of Arkansas to get a master's in business administration. That was at the University of Tulsa. Likewise, Joe Gorder, the chief executive of Valero, didn't end his education with his undergraduate career, from the University of Missouri–St. Louis. He, too, acquired an MBA—from Our Lady of the Lake University.
>
> When I looked just a few notches farther down the list of the Fortune 500 chief executives and took in the top 30, I spied the University of Central Oklahoma, the University of Pittsburgh, the University of Minnesota, Fordham, and Penn State—along with Cornell, Princeton, Brown, Northwestern, and Tufts. It was a profoundly diverse collection, reflecting the many routes to a corner office. (15)

What are your immediate thoughts after reading this passage?

How will this influence your college search and selection?

Our friend and colleague Jeff Selingo, in his book *Who Gets In and Why*, takes a close look into several admission offices around the country and provides helpful insight into how admission decisions are made:

> The anxiety about getting into a brand-name school starts with a single, fundamental principle believed by students and parents in top high schools: it matters *where* you go to college.
>
> It's a bedrock belief I have wrestled with for more than two decades of writing about higher education. I didn't go to a highly selective college, yet I'm surrounded by people who did—and many of them maintain that the name on their diploma has had a significant impact on their success in life.
>
> But CEOs and hiring managers tell me something different. When I wrote my last book, I spent time observing how executives from companies as large as IBM, Xerox, and Enterprise Rent-A-Car and as small as IDEO and Pinterest hire new college graduates. For the most part, I found that

job applicants' experiences and their skills matter more in hiring than their alma mater or major. The advice in that book was that how students go to college—from choosing a major and courses to finding internships—plays a much larger role in life after graduation than *where* they go to college.

Consider this: every year, some 1.8 million twentysomethings graduate from a four-year college. Only 54,000 of them receive a bachelor's degree from what we'd consider a selective college. Clearly, employers have more than 54,000 good jobs they need to fill each year with college graduates. (243)

What are your immediate thoughts after reading this passage?

How will this influence your college search and selection?

As you continue to explore your options and think about various educational settings, we recommend checking out *Colleges That Change Lives*, by Loren Pope, to learn about some of the most life-transforming colleges in our country. Pope writes,

> Teaching is an act of love. Students and professors develop a mentor relationship in class, and professors become students' hiking companions, intramural teammates, dinner hosts, and friends. Learning is collaborative rather than competitive; values are central; community matters. These colleges are places of great coherence, where the whole becomes greater than the sum of its parts. (4)

What are your immediate thoughts after reading this passage?

How will this influence your college search and selection?

2.4

College Bingo!

In the spirit of seeing a bigger landscape and learning more about options, we want you to find out where some people you know (or know of) went to college.

1. The CEO of your favorite national or international brand

2. Your principal / school head

3. Your town or city's mayor

4. Two or three of your neighbors or parents' friends

5. Your favorite science or math teacher

6. Your favorite history, foreign language, or English teacher

7. Your favorite athlete

8. The owner of your favorite local business

9. Your favorite actor or music artist

10. A state or federal legislator you respect

11. A famous person from your state

COLLEGE
BINGO

Located in New England	Located in South	Fewer than 10,000 undergrads
More than 30,000 undergrads	Private college	Public university
Mascot is an animal	Division I school	Division III school

OK. Now let's see if your answers cover all the squares in the college bingo card. If they do not, research other schools to complete the card. Compare your answers with a friend's or classmate's.

What did you learn?

What surprised you?

Is there a college or university on the list you had not heard of before?

2.5

Throw a Dart, Drop a Pin

When I (Rick) was a kid, I loved to place my finger on the globe in my room, spin it around, and see where my finger landed. I would research that city (clearly never Minneapolis) or country to learn about its people, culture, food, and history. Nerdy? Perhaps. But this is about you, not me.

Our friend and colleague Patrick Winter, associate vice chancellor of academic services and enrollment at the University of Nebraska–Lincoln, has a theory that if you were to throw a dart at a map of the United States, or enter coordinates into Google Earth and drop a pin online somewhere in this country, you would find a college within 100 miles where you could get in, meet a friend for life, engage with a professor who would support and encourage you, pick a major you would enjoy, and plug into a campus community where you could build a network and thrive during your undergraduate years and beyond. Give it a shot! (Just promise to be careful if you choose to blindfold yourself and throw darts.)

Let's say you dropped a pin on your house's location.

Draw a circle with a 100-mile radius from your house. What are your options inside the circle?

What if you expanded that to your entire state? Any state that borders your state?

Go online and search for the alumni magazine and student newspaper from some of those places. These are great resources, not only when you get to visiting colleges or making a final college choice, but also as you seek to keep an open mind and a broad perspective. In these publications, you will read about success stories, relationships that started on campus, and interesting, caring faculty and staff who make that school an incredible environment in which to learn, grow, and explore.

2.6

Check That Box

By this point, we hope we have established that colleges are looking for you. Again, the majority of schools in the country admit the majority of their applicants. If you are a sophomore or older, you can probably confirm this by going to your mailbox or checking your email and finding recruiting material sent to you by colleges. We have demonstrated the need for, and value of, keeping an open mind and being willing to consider colleges you may never have heard of before. And you have started to understand and articulate your *why* more clearly.

Now it's time to take some tangible steps.

Check that box. When you register to take standardized tests (including the PSAT, PreACT, SAT, and ACT) or when a survey is distributed in your high school for the purposes of college recruitment, you will see a box on the form asking you if you would like to share your contact information with colleges for the purpose of recruitment. We recommend you opt in by checking YES. This does mean you will be inundated with mail and email. Don't be annoyed. Receiving invitations for programs and events, hearing about scholarships, and simply seeing the incredible variety of colleges in our country will be a reminder that you have lots of options, need to continue refining your *why*, and should keep your focus on *experiences* instead of *process*.

Box up. Brochures are likely already starting to hit your mailbox. If you do not already have a good system (stacking them in a corner is not a system), take some time today to find three boxes.

Box 1: "Considering." This is where you or your family put brochures that match your why. Once a month you should go through the box to see what schools have fallen off your list and be sure you understand why that is the case.

Box 2: "For a Friend." When you receive a brochure from a school that is not a good match for you, think about who you know that may be interested in it, and pass it along. The college admission experience, if you'll let it, is an opportunity not only to learn more about yourself but also to grow in your relationships with your friends and family. Be a good friend and help them consider options and find a good college match.

And while you are at it, ask two or three of your best friends where they think you would be happy and successful in college. Have them walk you through their rationale. And, of course, return the favor—we are serious about that whole "be a good friend" thing.

Box 3: This one is essential: RECYCLE. Seriously. Do not be lazy and throw these things in the trash. Let's work together to save our planet one college brochure at a time.

Set your inbox. While this goes against our general life advice, be sure the email address you are using to communicate with colleges is as dull and generic as possible. Trust us: no admission dean wants to have to request a transcript from bigdawg32@gmail.com or lilmama12@icloud.com. You are going to receive (or already are receiving) an absurd amount of email. The good news is this is a regular reminder to stay open-minded and confident about having lots of choices. The bad news is that, after a while, receiving lots of email gets kind of annoying.

Here are some things to consider about email:

Do you want an email address for your college search that is separate from your personal account?

Do you want this to be a shared account with family members?

Do you want to create subfolders for sorting email, such as "considering," "visit," and "apply"?

As you move into the application phase, you may want to create separate folders for each individual college. Deadlines come quick, so staying organized is key. We will leave this up to you, but start figuring out your system now.

2.7

Add It Up

Everytime you get a postcard, letter, or brochure from a college, you can assume the college spent at least one dollar per page producing and mailing that piece. In other words, if a school sends you an eight-page publication, it invested at least eight dollars in trying to recruit you. Before you get rid of your recycling, do a quick count of the number of pages you received from colleges. Either write down amounts or keep a mental tally in your head over the next month.

The total is amazing, right? Schools go to great lengths to recruit and enroll students. They mail tens of thousands of pages annually to *prospects*, that is, to high school students they hope will consider attending.

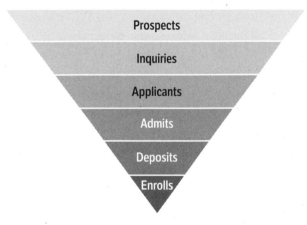

If you engage with schools through an online event, college fair, campus visit, or even by completing a web form, you move into the *inquiries* stage and generally their communications ramp up even more.

Whether through email or print pieces, the volume, quality, and specificity of material you receive from colleges increases as you move farther down the funnel. Our point in walking you through this diagram is partly to remind you that colleges are interested in you. However, it is also so that you will adopt a similar approach.

Colleges start broad. They search the nation and the world for the next class of students. Unfortunately, too many students start their search for colleges with too narrow a scope. They focus on just a few possible options and limit themselves as a result. Think instead like a dean of admission: start with lots of colleges and work from there.

2.8

Family Forward

My (Rick) family loves game night. One of my kids' favorite games is the classic board game Clue. If you are not familiar with it, the goal is to use the process of elimination to determine the *character* who committed the murder, the *weapon* the character used, and the *room* where the crime occurred. I know this does not sound family friendly, but bear with me.

First, you blindly draw a card from each category and put them in an envelope in the middle of the board. Then, by looking at the cards dealt to you, asking questions of the other players, and moving around the board to different rooms, you attempt to solve the mystery.

Until my daughter was 10 years old, she preferred to be the "holder of the cards," rather than actually play, because she could not handle the suspense.

As adults we are often in a state of suspense. When it comes to our kids, it can be difficult to be patient. Sometimes, in our well-intentioned desire to provide for them and have things go well, we want to control the game, "hold the cards," and know the outcome. As a parent in the college admission experience, think of yourself as a coach in the game of Clue. Help your student look at the letters, emails, and brochures they are receiving as *clues*. Encourage them to ask big questions about who they are and what they want. Give them the space and time to consider, refine, and record distinctions between what they *want* (would be nice) and they *need* in their college experience.

To extend the Clue metaphor, we understand there may be certain rooms you want them to consider. Rather than handing them certain cards or limiting the number of spaces they can move in any particular turn, prompt them to think about their school, community, teams, clubs, jobs, and other places and activities where they are involved and plugged in.

Like all good mysteries, the college search should be filled with twists, turns, discovery, new places, and interesting people. At times it might seem easier to simply pull the cards out of the envelope lying in the middle. After working with hundreds of students, we can tell you that, in a college search done right, that information comes only with time, effort, and a willingness to consider lots of options. Your job is to support them along the way.

2.9

Family Echo Chamber Escape

Helping your student keep an open mind and "see the entire board" requires perspective. In this chapter, we provided your student with a great deal of data to help them see how many amazing colleges and universities there are in our nation. Now it is your turn.

Write down the first seven college or university names that pop into your head.

1.

2.

3.

4.

5.

6.

7.

OK. Now write the names of colleges you know in your home state, the schools that you or someone in your family attended, the universities nationally known in your favorite sport, and any that rhyme with Stanvard. If you wrote down fewer than fifty names, we hope you will continue to broaden your knowledge of the many amazing colleges your student might visit, apply to, or attend.

Here is another activity we asked your students to do. Let's see if we can broaden your view even further.

In the list below, draw a line from the figure in the left column to its match in the right column.

~40   Number of schools included in *Colleges That Change Lives*

~55 percent   Average admit rate of Big 10 universities

~1,500   Number of American colleges with undergraduate populations under 1,000

~300   Number of American colleges starting with the letter *B*

~100   Number of colleges admitting less than 33 percent of applicants

~270   Number of American universities with undergraduate populations of more than 20,000

~980
                           Number of public community colleges

~64 percent   Average admit rate for four-year colleges

How did you do? Check the answers at the section's end and see.

Although your student may not always tell you this, as they can do a great job of pretending otherwise at times, the truth that is your influence on them is immense. We are convinced that a primary reason students stress about college admission is because they have a limited, inaccurate, or incomplete understanding of their options. Too often parents exacerbate that myopic viewpoint, rather than helping them see a bigger picture, keep an open mind, and support their exploration of a wide variety of schools.

Answers

Number of schools included in *Colleges That Change Lives* = ~40

Average admit rate of Big 10 universities = ~55 percent

Number of American colleges with undergraduate populations under 1,000 = ~1,500

Number of American colleges starting with the letter *B* = ~300

Number of colleges admitting less than 33 percent of applicants = ~100

Number of American universities with undergraduate populations more than 20,000 = ~270

Number of public community colleges = ~980

Average admit rate for four-year colleges = ~64 percent

We hope you will find this information deeply encouraging.

Take a moment to write one or two stats that surprised you.

What other numbers does this information make you want to investigate?

2.10

Come Together

We hope you have learned more about the landscape of higher education in the United States and the truly incredible number of great colleges and universities you can look into.

Take some time to compare the list of colleges you each came up with in the Echo Chamber exercises.

How many were overlaps, and why did you include those particular schools?

Which ones were different? Why were they on the list?

Are there schools on your list that you would definitely want to visit or know more about?

Are there colleges you wrote down but are not interested in pursuing for your college experience?

If the prompt was "Write down the five schools you are most interested in right now," what would be on your list? Actually, that is the prompt. We want you to talk through your top five at this point. Discuss why each one is listed, where you overlapped, and where you varied.

REMAPPING THE ADMISSION LANDSCAPE

You both did the exercise where you matched figures to higher education statistics (e.g., national admit rates and numbers of colleges in different categories).

Take turns sharing your reactions to the exercise.

What did you learn?

What surprised you?

What does that information prompt you to look into more?

Black out

Parents, rip the cover off brochures that come to your house in the next month. Then use a black felt-tip marker to blacken out the name of the college everywhere it appears. Give your student this job next month so that they get the satisfaction of doing some ripping too. Then take time to discuss these questions:

How does not knowing the name of a college change your perspective or opinions?

How do the questions you ask change when reviewing colleges this way?

Students, you did a lot more work in this chapter than your family did. Chapter 3 is all about being open and honest and staying committed to learning and growing together, so prepare now by sharing any other revelations or insights you gained from this chapter.

Chapter 3

Wedges of College Admission

Unlike the other chapters in this workbook where we have separate sections of activities for students and family members, this chapter is meant to be read and walked through together.

My (Rick's) son turned 12 this year. He is a "red-shirted" sixth grader now, and I'm seeing all the signs of a middle school boy. His feet are growing at a preposterous rate, he is sleeping later, and his body movements are shifting from little kid to some bizarre combination of convulsion and human worm.

I get it. I lived it. Still moderately disconcerting to witness, but I understand and recall (with cringe-worthy detail) those tween years.

My wife on the other hand . . . not so much. As a physical therapist, she understands the shifting circadian rhythms and physiological alterations resulting from accelerated growth. It's the communication piece that has her all twisted up.

Over the last year, our son's spike in one-word answers has only been rivaled by his decline in sharing both inconsequential and critically important information. Every abrupt utterance or omitted anecdote is my wife's death by a thousand cuts. Admittedly, this dialogue vacuum is juxtaposed with our 10-year-old daughter, who is an open book (actually, more like an open book series). One question and she's rolling from topic to topic with inflection, head flips, and body language any thespian would laud.

Is this chapter starting to feel painful, awkward, or extremely personal? Mission accomplished. Welcome to middle school. Welcome to my world. (If you need a primer or refresher before moving on, check out Trey Kennedy's middle schooler clips on YouTube.)

You, on the other hand, are no longer 12. (If you are 12 and reading this, go back to flipping cups or reading *Harry Potter* because it is far too early to think about college.) While there may not be many years between then and now, you are really in an entirely different stage. Driving, dating, working, and studying more, and jumping on trampolines less. This chapter is about bringing that same level of maturity and responsibility to your relationships during your college search.

Each year we have sat in awkward silence as students and family members argue about which schools are *good enough* and have heard comments like "All they talk about is college" and "Why are you telling us this just now?" and "I think college X would be great, but my sister went to Y university, and that's all my family is focused on."

Our goal is to help you avoid these situations by identifying the four primary wedges that divide, rather than unify, families in the admission experience. This starts with you committing to being proactive, honest, patient, and humble. A lot to ask, right? But you are not a middle schooler anymore. You are headed to college soon. You got this, and we have your back. The exercises in this chapter are broken into four parts, one for each wedge that we commonly see interfere with a unified college admission experience: *time*, *communication*, *money*, and *ego*. If you and your family will dedicate energy and attention as you go through these activities, and commit to really listening to one another and having open discussions even when it is uncomfortable, we are confident you will have a successful and enjoyable college admission experience.

3.1

College Conversation Creep (Time)

Students: Time, arguably, is our most valuable commodity. As a high school student, you are busy. Between school, friends, and outside activities, adding in something as big and important as the college admission experience can seem daunting or overwhelming. We get it.

As a student, we understand that your parents' seeming nonsequiturs like "Will you please put the ketchup back in the fridge, and be sure to ask Mrs. Thomas to write that recommendation for you" and "Remember, it's your grandma's birthday, so let's call her later. And how about that letter from UConn?" may appear random or annoying, but do not miss this important fact: all of that is coming from a place of deep love and affection.

We want to help you protect your time. Your college search is important, but it does not need to bleed into more of the week than necessary.

First, it's important to get a sense of how you are investing your time. This activity is a good primer for chapter 7, where we will again ask you to consider the activities you are participating in. If you already have this in an electronic calendar, you may not need it. Otherwise, use the table below, or create your own, to list and organize your commitments, the hours and days you are unavailable, and any corresponding notes that may be helpful. The top row is an example.

Activity	Days and hours	Notes
Work	4 p.m.–8 p.m. Tues. & Thurs.	Can't do those nights because of homework.

After looking this over and accounting for your time and obligations, what days and times would be best for you to have a weekly meeting about college? (*Hint*: Immediately following a long day at school plus work, or right after a sports practice, rarely leads to a productive conversation.)

Parents: We are with you. Our kids are growing up way too fast as well. For your family, time feels limited. Not only are your kids busy, but you also have your own responsibilities and full schedules. Meanwhile, you are seeing your time with your kids at home quickly elapsing.

It is tempting to seize on any opportunity you have to catch your student when they are awake and conversant so that you might squeeze even the smallest bit of information out of them about where things stand with their college search. Inevitably, this becomes tiring and frustrating for everyone, seeming to dominate every interaction. You think to yourself, "There has got to be a better way!" Well, you are right.

By the time the *spring of junior year* arrives, we strongly encourage your family to schedule a consistent thirty minutes each week when the college admission search and application experience is on the proverbial—and perhaps literal—table. In the fall of senior year, you may want to extend the time to an hour, but if you will isolate this time (and cancel or shorten judiciously), you can avoid the creep of college conversations.

Which day and time works best for your family? Take a look at everyone's schedules, and then put a weekly college meeting on the calendar for the next few months.

Put your own spin on this. We know some families who have done this after dinner on Sunday nights. Alternate who picks (or makes) dinner or dessert before or after the meeting. Approach is everything in college admission, so we hope you will see this as another opportunity to enjoy, learn, and grow closer to one another.

3.2

Making Meetings Matter (Time)

Finding a consistent time to meet is half the battle, so if you have accomplished that, pat yourselves on the back. Now it is important to ensure this valuable time together is not wasted or ineffective. This is a small fraction of your entire week. Make it count.

Set Ground Rules

We suggest you come up with two or three guidelines for your meetings that everyone can agree on in advance to help create a positive tone and united purpose. Perhaps your guidelines are "no sarcasm," "no crunchy food," and "no cell phones." That is up to you. However, one guideline we strongly suggest you set is keeping the focus on your family and your college search and selection, rather than on siblings, other students, or other families.

Meeting rules

1.

2.

3.

Agree on an Agenda

Begin each meeting by outlining what you hope to cover in your time together. Both student and parent should contribute at least one agenda item for discussion. Don't be overly ambitious. Stick to the most important topics for that week so that nobody leaves the meeting feeling overwhelmed. Keep it simple and enjoy.

Agenda items

1.

2.

3.

Next Steps

Before you leave the meeting, agree on and write down at least two actions steps you will each take before the next meeting.

Student

1.

2.

Parent

1.

2.

Meeting 1 sample agenda

- Agree before the meeting starts on mutually created ground rules.

- Discuss your individual *whys* from chapter 1.

- Both student and parent write the names of two to three schools you are currently interested in and the reason why. Where is their overlap and where is variance?

- *Action Steps*: In the spirit of keeping an open mind, commit to spending some time looking at the colleges from each other's list and revisiting them at the next meeting.

Other topics to include in the first month's meetings

- Discussion of brochures or emails you received recently. Why you are, or are not, interested.

- Are any colleges visiting your school or city in the weeks ahead? If so do you need to register in advance?

- Are you receiving information from the colleges you and your family are interested in hearing more about? If not, go to their admission website and complete the inquiry/prospect form.

What to bring and not to bring

- Bring brochures that have arrived in the mail that you would like to look at together.

- Bring questions about campus visit arrangements, majors offered, deadlines, scholarships, and so on.

- Bring SAT/ACT test dates and a plan for scheduling to take one or the other.

- Don't bring outdated stereotypes of colleges and universities based on your experiences twenty or thirty years ago.

- Don't bring a closed mind based on a college's cost, location, or mascot.

- Don't bring comparisons to other students, families, or older siblings.

3.3

Timeline Tracker (Time)

We have found it helpful for families to discuss, rather than assume, when and how to engage with college search. The following is an example framework for the four years of high school. It helps you identify what you should be planning for and thinking about in preparing to go to college. There is no magic formula or perfect way to approach this, so do not feel like you need to start setting up calendar reminders at this point. Add your own additional bullet points or develop your own timeline or calendar to help you consider, plan, and stay organized.

Freshman year

- Develop good study habits.

- Get involved. Learn about extracurricular activities. Try new things.

- Create a four-year academic plan with your school counselor.

- If you have excelled at a sport and think you may want to play at the college level, talk with your coach about when you should start planning for recruitment.

- Bottom line: be a good high school student!

Sophomore year

- Confirm or update your four-year academic plan with your school counselor.

- Begin informal visits to college campuses when traveling.

- Consider taking the PSAT and/or PreACT if your school offers them. Many test prep companies offer free diagnostic tests to determine which exam might be better for you.

- Determine whether test preparation during the summer will be valuable to you.

Junior year

- Take the PSAT in the fall.

- Meet with your school counselor about your college search and planning.

- Research college options.

- Meet with college representatives when they visit your high school.

- Visit colleges.

- Consider registering to take the ACT/SAT.

- Attend college workshops offered by your school's counseling office.

- Review your four-year academic plan and graduation and college entrance requirements.

- Begin scholarship searches.

- Complete the transcript release/waiver form for the NCAA if you are considering playing a sport at a Division I or II school.

- Work on an artistic portfolio or performance audition piece if you are applying to programs with these requirements.

- Attend college fairs.

- Ask junior teachers for college recommendations.

- During the summer, work on college essays and continue visiting colleges.

Senior year

- Meet with college representatives at your high school in the fall.

- Finalize a list of colleges to apply to.

- Retake the SAT/ACT if necessary.

- Submit all your applications by their deadlines.

- Submit financial aid forms—FAFSA (Free Application for Federal Student Aid) or CSS Profile—if required.

- Send enrollment deposit to the ONE college of your choice by its deadline.

- Write thank-you notes to those who wrote your letters of recommendation, and indicate where you are going to college. Hugs, fist bumps, and high fives are also encouraged.

- Notify the colleges you are not attending that you have committed to another school.

- Finish well and avoid "senioritis."

- Graduate!

3.4

Your Inner Circles (Communication)

Students: You are going to see friends posting where they visit and apply or talking about their "first choice" on social media. We have seen this backfire too many times, so our strong recommendation is to keep your college search close to your vest (or sweater, shirt, or hoodie) until you make a final choice.

Parents: The reality—especially in the age of social media—is that chatter about colleges can have unintended consequences. When it comes to applying and paying for college, your family (and those of your friends and colleagues) understandably feels a disconcerting combination of pride, nervousness, and lack of control. As a result, at athletic games, parties, or online, you will come across many conversations about who was or was not admitted to certain colleges or speculation about why the class salutatorian did not receive that major merit award. Too often such talk leads to hurt feelings, upset children, and unchecked rumors.

We will discuss this further later in the book, but since you do not control how admission decisions play out, and because money, emotions, and many other factors shift and influence a final college choice, it is important to limit your sharing of information about the college search to people you trust and know are completely on your team.

Draw It Out

The circles below are there for you to write inside them the names of those who belong to the inner circle of your college search. (Yes, it's OK to put someone right on the line or just outside it.)

Students: Think about whom you trust to provide honest feedback, to review your essays, to provide insight on *what you are known for*, to listen to your *why*, and speak to your thought and decision-making process; those who will celebrate with you when you receive offers of admission and console and encourage you when disappointments arise. Write their names in the circle.

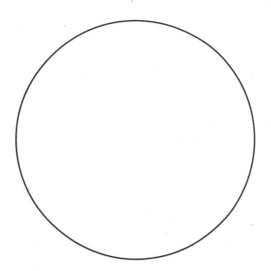

Parents: Think about whom you trust to keep the details of your family's college search private. Who has been through this experience recently and can offer accurate information and straightforward feedback and support? Write their names in the circle.

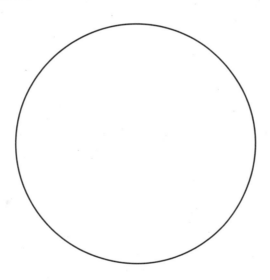

In one of your initial weekly family meetings, talk about the names in the circles above and why each person is listed. Trust and communication go hand in hand. Students, be honest with your parents about what you are and are not comfortable with them posting, commenting, or sharing about your college admission experience.

3.5

Family Pronoun Test (Communication)

We know that you love your kids . . . but *you are not them*. Every year admission offices receive calls like this: "*We* were deferred from your college. I know that you've received *our* transcript and supplement (because I made him give me his log-in info), and I see from your website that you don't use an interview or additional letters of recommendation in the process, but I'm going to have two of my business associates email on his behalf anyway." Admission staff often see students slump down in their chairs at information sessions (and a few even get up and walk out) when a father launches into question number seven, or a student slips to the back of the tour when mom grills the tour guide incessantly.

We are confident that you do not want to be an example of what not to do in a future admission presentation or article, so let's see if any of this sounds familiar.

Have you recently said . . .

We are taking the SAT next weekend.

OR

Our favorite visit was to Amazing College.

OR

Let's nail that calculus exam so *we* can get the A.

Periodically checking your pronouns is one of the easiest ways to ensure you are avoiding the communication wedge. It will also help you ask questions about your student's college essays and make helpful edits or suggestions rather than being tempted to rewrite the essay with words like *lugubrious* or *obsequious*. The communication wedge is real but avoidable. In a short year or two, *they* will be on a college campus. *They* will need to be able to advocate and navigate for themselves. Watching your pronouns allows you to step back without stepping away.

While pronouns can be divisive if misused, they also have the ability to keep your family learning and unified. How can you use *we*, *our*, and *us* to encourage and bond, rather than as a wedge?

Here are three uses that we hope you'll consider committing to:

1. We can listen with curiosity and a desire to understand one another.

2. We can look beyond what we see and keep an open mind through the college search.

3. We can talk about money openly, honestly, lovingly, early, and often.

What other *we* actions can you take to help your family stay on the same page?

4. We

5. We

6. We

3.6

College Costs (Money)

Any admission dean, financial aid director, or college counselor can share countless painful stories about families coming to their office in tears in April of the student's senior year of high school either holding a financial aid letter like a weight or using it as a tissue. The student has been offered admission, bought the college hoodie, and posted on their social media profile that they are going. Now, however, the reality of paying for college is setting in, and the tension within the family is palpable.

Does that sound uncomfortable and awkward? Trust us—it is way worse in real life. Do not end up in one of those offices!

Parents, we understand that one of the reasons college admission is stressful is because it combines two things in your life you often think and worry about the most: *your kids* and *your money*. While we cannot change that fact, your family can avoid the money wedge by understanding the costs and being willing to engage in early, open, and honest conversations about paying for college.

Let's start with college costs. If paying for college were like buying a car, the truth is much of the stress would be eliminated. You would look at the sticker price, determine if you had the cash to pay, and, if not, calculate what a monthly loan would look like. Throw in a little bit of haggling with the fictitious "manager in the back," and you are rolling—literally.

Unfortunately, that is not how paying for college works. Let's start with the fact that the price published online or in the literature you pick up on your visit to campus is often not the actual amount you end up paying. Already confused? Don't worry; we will get to that.

College Cost Calculator

Ready to see how this plays out? Search online for five of the schools you are interested in visiting or applying to. Create a spreadsheet or use the table below to record their published costs. For the purposes of this exercise be sure to include at least one public and private college. Remember not to rule out a school based on the price you see online or assume the lowest total will be the one that will ultimately cost the least.

College name					
Website					
Tuition and fees					
Books and supplies					
Housing and meals					
Travel					
Personal expenses					
Total cost of attendance					
Notes					

Note: Most two-year and four-year colleges will display the total cost for the school year (fall and spring semesters combined); however, in the Notes row you should indicate whether the costs listed are per semester or per year.

What are your initial reactions to the information you found?

What surprised you?

What other questions do you have after seeing these details?

As we said, the total cost of attendance (COA) is not exactly the price you will pay. In the exercises that follow, we will help you better understand the factors that go into determining more accurate expected costs for your family, facilitate important conversations to help you avoid the money wedge, and ensure you will not be the family crying in the dean's office in April (tears + awkwardness = wedge).

3.7
Net Price Knowledge (Money)

Now that you have COA down, let's check out some of the other key acronyms in the college financial aid world. Search online to find the net price calculator (NPC) for the schools you listed in your table or spreadsheet in section 3.6. You will find some NPCs are fancier than others, but each college in the United States is required to have one on their site. By entering your most current financial information in different colleges' NPCs, you will be able to see what students from families with similar financial circumstances paid to attend that particular institution in the previous year.

Here is some of the information you will be asked to gather and enter:

- Previous year's tax return data
- Adjusted gross income (found on tax return)
- Family context (e.g., any other children in college, custodial and non-custodial parental information)
- Business owners—accurate income and assets
- For divorced/separated/never-married parents, some schools will want information from both parents, regardless of marital status. In cases where one parent is not and has not been a part of the student's life, schools will need some details to waive the requirement
- Complex situations (health issues and medical expenses, disasters, deaths, etc.)

Now update your spreadsheet or use the table below.

What are your biggest takeaways from your research and comparisons?

How does having this information change the questions you have about financial aid in general or specifically for the colleges you are considering?

College name	Published COA	Net price (estimate)	Notes/questions, including a known or likely scholarship, grant, work-study offer, or loan

3.8

Limitations, Conditions, Expectations (Money)

You will hear college counselors and admission officers talk a lot about students finding a good academic, cultural, and geographic fit. Increasingly, however, it is critical to ask questions and initiate an early dialogue to help assess financial fit.

There is usually a difference between what a family *can* afford and what they are *willing to* pay for. That principle is true in life in general (think houses, cars, clothes), and it is, and should be, true for education as well. Parents too often feel guilty about outlining *limitations, conditions, and expectations*, but you will significantly help your family's admission experience if you are willing to explain how paying for college ties into your overall financial picture.

You do not have to get into specifics about your salary, but we hope you will use this as an opportunity to tell your student about your retirement goals, annual taxes, or mortgage rates. We know college is a big investment. We want you to be confident about every dollar you spend on higher education. If you will discuss your financial goals and responsibilities, they will both respect and appreciate how to incorporate that information into their college search and selection. Honesty and openness will ensure your conversation about paying for college does not come across as limiting but rather as instructive and rooted in love.

List Limitations

Particularly in states with strong public university systems, we often hear families say, "I am willing to pay for any of our state schools or the equivalent price if my daughter chooses an out-of-state public or private school."

What limits, if any, do you have on paying for college?

Are your limits general, or are they at all linked to geography or to what your student chooses as a major?

When you think about paying for college, are you looking at the first year only, two years, or a four-year investment?

List and discuss any limits you may have that pertain to financing college.

1.

2.

3.

How does paying for college factor into other financial obligations and goals, long-term plans for retirement, and overall lifestyle?

Based on other financial considerations, plans, and family financial goals or obligations, are you able to settle on an annual or total dollar figure that you are willing to invest in your student's college education?

Consider Conditions

We have heard many students say things like "My parents will not pay for a school south of DC" or "They have already told me they will not pay for schools outside the US" or "They will pay $30,000 a year for college X but are not willing to pay that same amount for Y university."

List any *conditions* you have or think you would like to explore further.

1.

2.

3.

Enumerate Expectations

My (Rick's) sister-in-law grew up in North Carolina. She initially attended the University of Wyoming on a partial soccer scholarship. When she decided to transfer, my father-in-law told her he would pay for a North Carolina public university or the equivalent amount elsewhere. She chose Clemson University, which, for those keeping score at home, is not a North Carolina public university. At that point, she understood how much she was going to need to contribute by working or taking loans (which we cover in 3.9).

Consider and discuss

Is there a flat amount or percentage of college costs that you expect your child to pay each semester or year?

Do you expect your child to work and save a certain amount of money to contribute to their tuition prior to entering college?

Do you expect them to work during the academic year in college or contribute a certain amount or percentage after their first year of school?

We understand that discussing money may feel a bit uncomfortable. However, each year we hear parents of seniors talk about what they *wish* they could do financially or express guilt about not being able to pay more. Often, we come to learn they have never discussed these matters directly with their student. Trust us: students appreciate being invited into these honest conversations.

3.9
Lowdown on Loans (Money)

Here are a few facts about student loans:

1. Seventy percent of college students take out loans to help finance their education, according to MarketPlace.org, https://www.marketplace.org /2019/09/30/70-of-college-students-graduate-with-debt-how-did-we-get -here/.

2. While the media and politicians are quick to talk about the trillion-dollar college loan problem in our country, the average college student loan debt in the United States is approximately $30,000.

3. The average starting salary for four-year college graduates is approximately $50,000.

4. The average monthly loan payment for recent college graduates is $393, according to the Motley Fool, https://www.fool.com/student-loans/heres -average-student-loan-payment-how-lower-yours/.

Now that you have a sense of net price and have discussed conditions, limitations, and expectations, loans may also need to be part of your conversation and financing equation. Expand your table from 3.7 by filling in the table below. In order to estimate a loan amount, deduct how much your family is willing or able to pay from the estimated net price you calculate for each school: net price minus any variance based on limitations, conditions, expectations = cost gap and estimated loan amount. *Note*: These are rough numbers at this point that do not account for tuition increases, other scholarships, grants, and so on.

College name					
COA					
Estimated net price					
Notes (accounting for limitations, conditions)					
Need-based aid					
Cost gap and estimated loan amount					
Notes					

Direct PLUS Loans (also known as Parent PLUS Loans) allow parents to borrow directly from the US Department of Education; they can take out a loan amounting to the cost of attendance (determined by the school) minus any financial aid received. This means, in some cases, parents are borrowing thousands or tens of thousands of dollars to finance their student's education.

Take time as a family to discuss your philosophy on, experience with, or personal observations of the risks and benefits of taking out loans, and discuss your annual or overall tolerable loan amount.

How does your conversation about loans complement discussions about limitations, conditions, and expectations?

Students, will the information you now have impact how you make and save money in high school?

What questions does this information help you formulate for colleges related to opportunities for on-campus jobs or the prospects for (and salaries associated with) internships or co-ops while in college?

What questions does this information bring up for you as you talk to colleges about return on investment, careers, majors, starting salaries, and how they help their students pursue employment opportunities during and after college?

How do you think laying out financial information at this point can help make paying for college a joint and unified effort, rather than a divisive or tension-filled problem?

3.10

Ego Exam (Ego)

We know this chapter has already asked a lot of you—initiating intentional conversations with your family, setting aside time each week to focus on something that may seem unnecessary at this point in high school, and having real and serious conversations about the uncomfortable topic of money. To be honest there are a lot of adults (a lot) who do not have the will or skill to handle all of that.

Now you are ready to tackle the final wedge: ego. Don't skip over this if you are either insulted by the title or convinced you are a generally humble person. To be honest, when we say *ego*, we are really just urging you to keep perspective. This wedge shows up at various points for different families, so, students, let's start with some self-examination.

Checking Your Ego

Students

When you receive college letters, brochures, or invitations to visit campus, is your first thought, "Does this school match my *why*?" Or is it "Is this place good enough for me?" or "How would it look if I went there?"

If you lean more toward the second or third thought, where is your concept of good coming from, and who are you concerned about impressing or pleasing?

How can you put checks in place when you receive advertisements from schools so that you remain objective, open, and thinking independently?

Are you willing to consider colleges you have not heard of or ones nobody in your family or school has attended before? Why or why not?

What role are college rankings or the opinions of others playing in your college search? In other words, do you believe your identity or worth is tied to getting into a specific school?

Are you open to the college suggestions that your counselor, teachers, coaches, and family members make? When they say, "I really think you would love college X," how do you respond? And why?

Colleges publish a middle 50 percent admit range for test scores. For instance, let's say a college shows that last year's class scored between 1200 and 1300 on the SAT. (The national average is ~1000.) This means 25 percent of the admitted class scored below a 1200, and 25 percent were admitted with a score above 1300. If your SAT score is in a school's top quartile, does your perception of that school change? Why?

When a family member wants you to visit or apply to your state flagship school, the college closest to your house, or their alma mater, are you willing to legitimately run those through your *why* filter to see whether or not they are a good match? Why or why not?

Parents

What defines a "good" school in your mind?

Are you attaching your success as a parent, or your image in general, to where your child is admitted or ultimately enrolls?

Have you committed to keeping an open mind and letting go of stereotypes of certain colleges?

Are you open to checking any preconceived notions about specific schools, regions of the country, or types of colleges against data and current student insight?

Will you celebrate every admit your student receives and not reserve excitement for the school you are most hopeful they will attend?

We don't have any gold stars to hand out, but we appreciate you participating. Just being willing to walk through these questions and discuss your honest thoughts means you're acing this course so far.

3.11

FOR Your Family (Ego)

Jeff Henderson has worked for some of Atlanta's most iconic brands, including the Atlanta Braves and Chick-fil-A. Recently he launched his own company geared toward helping others embrace their mission and grow their brand. In his book *Know What You're FOR*, he asks the reader to consider two fundamental questions: *What are you known for? What do you want to be known for?*

Family and student, take ten to fifteen minutes to write down these answers. Feel free to go into separate rooms to do this, and be sure everyone participates.

What are you known for?

What do you want to be known for?

Once you come back together, have each person share what they believe the others are *known for.* Students, if the answers you receive from others about what you are *known for* vary from how you responded, consider how that feedback can help you in high school and as you search for colleges.

Now turn to the second question: *What do you want to be known for?* Allow each person to talk about their answer, and have a brief discussion about any gaps between desire and current reality.

3.12

Wedge Wrap-up

Now that you have identified and worked through all of the wedges of college admission, we would like you to have a family conversation about these questions:

What does success look like for your family in the college admission experience?

Do your family's actions, words, attitudes, and time spent together reflect that goal?

Where is the gap?

What role do you need to play in bringing these closer together?

As you move forward together in your college admission experience and the other exercises in this workbook, we hope you will use these questions as a framework.

Part II

Chapter 4

Creating a College List

Imagine that you and your family are going out for dinner to celebrate a special occasion or accomplishment. How do you decide where to go given everyone's different tastes, opinions, or dietary restrictions? Or perhaps your family is buying a new car or is in the market for a new house. What approach do you take to narrow down your many options? If there were only a handful of restaurants, car models, or houses for sale, this might be a fairly simple choice. But what if there were more than four thousand options? Would you find that encouraging or daunting? As you learned in chapter 2, you have thousands of colleges and universities to choose from in this country.

While that realization may feel exciting and full of opportunity for some, it often feels overwhelming and uncertain to others. The reality is that most students and families fall somewhere in between these two extremes.

Regardless of where you are on that continuum, it is important to know you are not alone. College is a big deal, and the truth is that choosing one is often exciting and overwhelming simultaneously. We also understand that choosing a college is likely to be one of the first significant decisions of your life, so the stakes can feel high. Over the years, we have found that students who keep focused on choices and options, buy in to the reality that there is no one *right* decision or *perfect* school, remain committed to asking good questions and being honest with themselves along the way, and view this as an experience instead of a process ultimately discover tons of great college matches academically, financially, and socially. The truth is your college search should not be linear. Doing this right means being open to an evolving understanding of your hopes, goals, and needs, so expect your college list to expand, narrow, and shift.

"Okay," you might be wondering: "So where do I start?" The truth is that you are already farther ahead of most students because of the work you did in chapter 1 by answering "*why?*" Using that answer and starting to clarify the experience you want to have in college is exactly how you build a list of schools to research, visit, and apply to. Our goal is to provide you with the questions to ask and the tools to use to figure out which schools are possible matches.

There are many great online search tools (such as those listed in Resources at the end of this book) that will allow you to refine your college list. In order to use these tools effectively, you will need to have a general idea of what you are looking for, and that is going to require some groundwork. The exercises and facilitated conversations in this chapter are designed to help you engage, discover, and identify a thoughtful array of schools to explore. We ask you to think critically about the role of rankings and other influences as you build your list, and we encourage you to take a balanced and intentional approach in your efforts to narrow your options. By the end of this chapter, you will have specified your initial criteria and sorted your list into *reach*, *target*, and *likely* schools.

4.1

Influencer Impact

It is impossible to build a college list in a void. We are undeniably influenced by factors in our environment and the individuals and groups in our lives. As you begin to add colleges and universities to your list to research, visit, and apply to, it is helpful to consider the impact of these influencers and how their views inform your experience.

Below is a list of common influencers. For each one, give a rating from *0 = no influence* to *10 = highly influential*. Add your own individuals, groups, or factors at the bottom.

Influencer	Influence rating (0–10)	Notes (why?/how?)
Parents/guardians		
Grandparents / extended family		
Siblings		
Teachers		
Friends		
Teammates		
Cost		
College rankings		
College selectivity		
College reputation		
Work manager		
Coach / club sponsor		

In the Come Together section at the end of this chapter, take time to share your thoughts with your family about how and why these people or factors will impact your search.

4.2

Resource Reliability

As you begin to research colleges, you will find a great deal of information about colleges and admission online, in various books and articles, or on social media. In fact, there is so much information that it can often be challenging to discern what is valuable and accurate and what is rumor, conspiracy theory, or random opinion. Below is a list of common sources of information about schools and admission. For each, give a rating from *0 = completely objective* to *5 = highly subjective*. Add your own resources at the bottom and rate them as well.

Resource	Subjectivity rating (0–5)	Notes (how/why?)
High school counselor		
College website		
College guidebooks		
Reddit, etc.		
Friends		
Social media		
Family		
Admission staff		
Media		
College visit		

Discuss your responses with family and others who support you. And keep these ratings in mind as you continue to weigh your options and gather information about the colleges you are considering.

4.3
Word Choice

In the list below, circle the words or phrases that best apply to your ideal college or university, and cross out those that do not resonate with or have importance to you. Take your time and be honest. This may seem simple, but thinking through these priorities is a key step as you move forward. Remember that it is OK not to circle *or* cross out an item; that simply indicates you do not feel strongly about it.

Academic support	Coed school
Close to home	Cutting-edge academics
Urban	Socially conservative
Intramural sports	Famous for science
Famous professors	Intense
Competitive students	Accessible professors
Personal	Campus life
Cold	Graduate programs
Large classes	School spirit
Cosmopolitan	Friendly
Few requirements	Research oriented
Many international students	Small classes
Core curriculum	Classes taught by professors
Religious atmosphere	Intellectual
Unconventional students	Single-sex school

Leadership opportunities

Many outdoor activities

Rural

Many cultural activities

Ethnically diverse student body

Fraternities and sororities

Everyone knows you

Dress-conscious students

Ivy League

Active in arts and music

Personal atmosphere

Subdued social life

Athletics are important

Strong study abroad

Warm

Safe

Liberal arts

Admission test optional

Preprofessional programs

Student activism

Transportation

Reasonable cost

What is missing? Add your own words to this list and come back to it as you receive brochures and emails from schools, visit campuses, and get ready to apply to college.

4.4
Needs and Wants

We hope you are beginning to zero in on the aspects of a college that are nonnegotiable or negotiable for you. As an example, maybe you know you want to study a specific major, play a certain sport, or be within a day's drive from home. If you would not consider a college that doesn't meet these criteria, then that is a *need*. Other aspects might be more negotiable; perhaps you would prefer to be in a college town, but you are open to a rural campus; or you would rather not have fraternities and sororities be part of the college experience, but this is not a deal breaker. These are *wants*. Finally, there are factors in your search that will fall into the "it would be *nice to have*" category: a winning football team, an accordion club, or proximity to a big airport for direct flights home.

Our hope is that you can start to identify and classify these different needs and wants as early as possible in your college search but that you will also be open to shifts as you learn more about schools and yourself. Write your needs, wants, and nice-to-haves in the three circles below, and revisit your answers as your college search progresses.

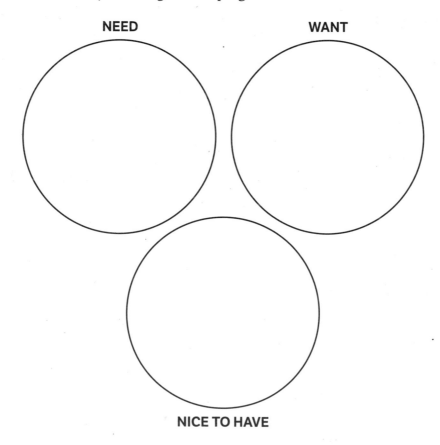

NEED   **WANT**

NICE TO HAVE

4.5

Criteria Grid

Visualizing and locking in on your criteria is an invaluable way to help build your list of schools. Consider each category in the table below and circle or highlight the items that are appealing to you. Similarly, cross out the items or boxes that you feel strongly are not for you.

Size	Small, 1,000–3,500 students	Medium, 3,500–8,000 students	Large, 8,000–15,000 students	Enormous, >15,000 students
Setting	Rural	Suburban	Urban with quad	Urban without quad
Region	East	South	Midwest	West
Type of school	University = made up of several smaller colleges with specific areas of study. Also offers graduate programs.	College = liberal arts program that requires study across the disciplines, with a major area of focus	*Specific type* • Business • Technical • Arts • Single gender	*Religious* • Catholic • Jesuit • Quaker • Jewish • Other
Programs	Co-op = combines classroom learning with hands-on, real-world work experience	*Internships* • Institutional support • Formal programs • Availability • Class year of eligibility	*Study abroad* • Summer • Semester • Junior year abroad • Required	3/2 program = combined or dual-degree programs in engineering
Academics	*Academic support* • Peer/professional tutors • Drop-in centers • Teaching assistants	*Core requirements* • How many classes? • How restrictive?	*Majors and minors* • Ability to create your own • Ease of double major	*Other considerations* • Freshman seminars • Workload • Faculty-student ratio
Students	*Politics* • Liberal • Conservative • Interested and active • Uninterested	*Disposition* • Happy • Sophisticated • Outgoing • Independent	*Academics* • Hardworking • Competitive • Engaged • Cooperative	*Interests* • Outdoors • Athletics • Arts/music/theater • Community service

Athletics	Division I Division II Division III Intramural	School spirit Facilities	*Students* • On teams • Physically fit • Rabid fans • Nonathletic	*Most competitive teams*:
Facilities	*Library* • Place to study • Place to gather • Place to get information	*Classrooms* • Technology • Appearance	*Student Center* • Food service • Place to gather	*Dorms* • Housing guaranteed? Required? • Theme dorms • Suites/singles/doubles • % of students on campus
Other criteria	Campus activities	Accessible	*Financial aid* • Need blind? • Meet full need?	Merit scholarships
	Selectivity • Admit rate • Yield = % accepted who attend	Greek life	Diversity	Male-to-female ratio
	Surrounding area	Retention rate	Four-year graduation rate	Dining halls

Source: Adapted from Allison Matlack of Matlack Consulting, https://www.matlackeducational consulting.com/.

4.6

Free Association

Another great way to start building your college list is to write down the schools you know about or have visited in the past. By doing this, you are able to check in on your preconceived notions and past experiences.

In the table below, write down colleges that come to mind and how you are familiar with them (e.g., friend attended, sports team, summer camp, drove through campus, parents talk about it). In the final column, write the first three words that come to mind when you think of this college. Don't overthink it. Just record your initial thoughts.

Name of college	How do you know it?	Three descriptive words

Once you are done, take some time to discuss these schools and your perceptions with a friend or classmate. See if they agree with your impressions of the schools or have additional information or opinions that may lead you to ask more questions or investigate further. Later in this chapter we will ask you to do this again with your family members in the Come Together section.

4.7
Mind Map

Georgia Tech has developed a mind map to help students think through their interests. Use the blank map in the figure below, draw your own, or go online and create one using a mapping software program. Mind mapping is an exercise where you take one big idea and break it up into smaller parts. Doing this for your college search may help you see any larger themes that could influence your choice of schools to apply to. Fill in the blank diagram to map your interests and potential careers relating to those interests.

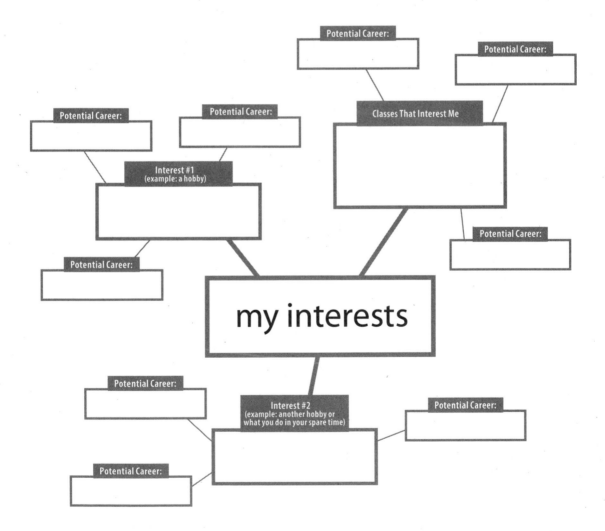

4.8
Funnel

As you research colleges, visit, revisit, and refine your list, the number of schools that show up as best matches will begin to narrow. In working with students, we have found it is helpful to visualize this process and to have a record of where you started and a window into where you are headed. Just like colleges start with a large number of prospective students, and then progressively work down to their final entering class, you should do the same.

Track your progress in narrowing by filling in each tier in the funnel diagram with the prospective schools on your list. As shown in the example, the widest tier should be colleges you plan to research. Based on that exploration, some schools will move down to the next tier, where you will inquire, requesting more information about those schools. Next, list the schools you want to visit (either in-person or virtually). After you take these steps, the number of schools will narrow to those to which you are applying. The next level is the schools you are accepted to—ultimately pointing to where you plan to enroll. Trust us: you will get to that point.

4.9

Financial Fit

As you know, earning a college degree can be an expensive endeavor. However, as you are learning, the landscape of colleges, and their associated costs, vary widely. Your goal is to find schools that make financial sense for your family. This will mean continuing to examine your financial situation and thinking critically about the role that college costs will play as you are building your list. Our friend and colleague Cicily Shaw, director of college counseling at Boston Trinity Academy, explains that "many families do not consider financial fit early in the college application process. Only when financial aid is awarded, do families see the gravity of affording a college education." She suggests that financial fit be considered when students begin to develop their application list.

This activity will help explain why it is essential to figure out your financial fit by answering three questions.

- What does *financial fit* mean?

- Why is it important to consider financial fit?

- How do you determine financial fit?

What Is Financial Fit?

Finding financial fit takes a bit of sleuthing, but it can be determined. Often, a college's sticker price can be intimidating, and many families will overlook a good college option because of the cost (as we outlined in exercise 3.6). More goes into finding the financial fit of an institution than merely looking at its sticker price. There are ways to determine ballpark figures to see if a college is affordable. Estimating financial fit provides families with information about the college's affordability. Collegedata.com offers the following questions to consider as you determine an institution's financial fit.

Does the college have . . .

- a history of providing generous gift aid (grants and scholarships)?

- a history of substantially meeting students' financial need? (Many colleges don't.)

- a policy of not reducing gift aid after freshman year? (Some colleges do.)

- a history of providing generous merit aid? (This is aid not based on financial need.)
- a history of low student debt upon graduation?

Why Is It Important to Determine Financial Fit?

Determining financial fit is essential because families should be leery of taking on significant debt for an undergraduate degree. College is an investment, so families must decide what a reasonable college investment will look like for them. Did you know that, according to the Federal Reserve, more than half of young adults who went to college in 2018 took on debt? About 69 percent of students from the class of 2018 took out student loans, graduating with an average debt balance of **$29,800**, according to StudentLoan Hero.com.

When considering the amount of debt a family is willing to take on, students should also be aware of earning potential with a bachelor's degree. PayScale (www.payscale.com/college-roi/methodology) provides families with a snapshot of return on investment for individual institutions. According to the US Bureau of Labor Statistics, the median weekly earnings of full-time wage-earning and salaried workers aged 25 and older was $909 in the second quarter of 2017. Full-time workers without a high school diploma had median weekly earnings of $515, compared with $718 for high school graduates (no college) and $1,189 for those with a bachelor's degree. Full-time workers with advanced degrees (professional or master's degree and above) had median weekly earnings of $1,451.

How Do You Determine Financial Fit?

There are several online tools families can use to help determine financial fit. The financial health of an institution significantly affects how much financial aid that institution can offer. Families should consider five key figures when determining financial fit.

1. **Four-Year Cost of Attendance**
   This amount will include tuition, room and board, mandatory student fees, and books and supplies for four years.

2. **Four-Year Graduation Rate**
   What percentage of students graduate in four years? Adding time to any degree program beyond four years can mean more out-of-pocket expenses.

3. **Average Financial Aid**

   Many colleges disclose their average financial aid and scholarships awarded to students. Be mindful, though, that these are averages and may not apply, depending on your family's individual financial situation.

4. **Net Price**

   The actual amount a family will pay after any discounts, scholarships, or grants. To get a general figure, families should use the net price calculator described in exercise 3.6.

5. *Hechinger Report* **Stress Score**

   The Hechinger Report developed the Financial Fitness Tracker. This tool may be helpful for families in determining the financial health of an institution. With the close of many small private colleges, discovering an institution's financial health is necessary to ensure that families have carefully thought out the possibility of institutions closing because of financial stress.

   According to *The Hechinger Report*, the scores draw on publicly available data provided by the National Center for Education Statistics and show the estimated amount of financial stress on an institution after the 2019–2020 academic year, without attempting to quantify the still-uncertain effects of the coronavirus crisis. The tracker makes no determination about whether a school is more or less likely to close or merge with another institution, nor does it assess the quality of education an institution offers or its competitiveness against other institutions (tuitiontracker.org/fitness/methodology.html).

Determining Financial Fit

To complete the chart below, use the following resources:

Payscale ROI Report: https://www.payscale.com/college-roi

Financial Fitness Tracker: https://tuitiontracker.org/fitness/

NetPrice Calculator: https://npc.collegeboard.org/

Institution name	Cost of attendance	Four-year graduation rate	Net price	Average financial aid	*Hechinger Report* stress score

Source: Adapted from Cicily Shaw, director of college counseling at Boston Trinity Academy.

4.10

Rank the Rankings

If you are a college football or basketball fan, you know that the way teams are ranked is not purely based on their win-loss record. Because not all schools have the chance to play one another each season, the experts use a variety of metrics, algorithms, and a healthy dose of personal opinion and bias. Not a sports fan? Go find a list of best songs, bands, YouTube videos, or something else you are interested in. Inevitably, you are going to disagree with the list, at least in part. If you are like most people, you will pretty quickly also question and criticize the source, "C'mon! Seriously? Who is the idiot that came up with these?"

In the world of colleges, there is no shortage of rankings. Publications will rank schools by "the friendliest," "the greenest," or the best in a state or region. When you see these lists, especially if a college sends you something boasting about its status, we hope you will raise one eyebrow before taking the objectivity of any number at face value. We hope you will ask questions like these:

How did the source arrive at this ranking?

Who is putting this together, and what is their motivation?

And most importantly, do I really care?

Let's start with a well-known example of commercial rankings. Go online and search for "U.S. News and World Report College Rankings and Methodology" (https://www.usnews.com/education/best-colleges/articles/how-us-news-calculated-the-rankings). You will find links where you can see the percentage weight assigned to variables in calculating these rankings.

What did you find?

What did you think was a valid and helpful metric to use?

What did you see that surprised you?

What variables would you want to add, reorder, or eliminate?

Does it matter to you that a president from one college looks favorably on another, especially accounting for intercollegiate competition?

Is a school's ability to pay a faculty member $2,000 more annually ($244/month or $8/day) of consequence to your college search and choice?

Based on the way these rankings are formulated and the motivations you might infer their producers had for creating them, what role will they play in your researching, visiting, or applying to college?

4.11

The Rank King

Here's the thing. As we have said and will continue to reiterate, your college search and selection is just that—*yours*. To be honest, we think you are more capable of creating a worthy ranking system than the data analysts working at any of these companies. And, beyond that, you know what *you* care about. They do not.

If you work well with lists, hierarchies, or ratings, then you are likely going to love this activity. We want you to think about what criteria are important to you and rank schools based on your own preferences and research, rather than someone else's. In the table below, or one of your own making, list the factors that matter to you in your college search; then, for each college, rate it from *1 = not impressed* to *10 = nearly ideal*. At the end, you can total your ratings if you wish or give more weight to those factors that matter to you more than others. The most important part is that you will know why you assigned the ratings, recognize the value you gave each, and understand how these numbers can help you build a list of colleges.

We do not want to lead you too much, but here are some examples of factors you might include: *location, faculty accessibility, social scene, distance from home, safety, housing, internships,* and *academic major.* You may want to refer to exercise 4.5 for other factors to consider.

College	Criteria #1	Criteria #2	Criteria #3	Criteria #4	Criteria #5	Criteria #6	Criteria #7	Criteria #8	Criteria #9	Total score

Based on what you included as factors, you may realize you have more research to do. As you move forward in your college search, revisit, re-rank, and re-weight your list.

The other exercises in this chapter have helped you identify what you are looking for in a college and supported you in building your list. Ideally, you will arrive at a list of six to ten schools that answer your *why*. We advise that you break down your final group as follows.

- Two to three "reach" schools where your grades and scores put you below the average admitted student.

- Three to five "target" schools where your profile aligns with the average admitted student (giving you roughly a fifty-fifty chance of getting in).

- One to two "likely" schools where you are well above the average admitted student.

Take a look at Example College's admission profile to see how your academic background fits it.

EXAMPLE COLLEGE (Home of the Fighting Ex's!) Admitted Class Profile for 2020–21

HIGH SCHOOL GRADE POINT AVERAGE
Middle 50 percent of admitted first-year students: 3.74–4.00
Note: If the top end of their middle 50 percent is 4.00 (or higher in some cases), you know the school must either recalculate grades or add weight to grade point averages.

STANDARDIZED TESTS
SAT middle 50 percent of admitted first-year students: 1320–1430
ACT middle 50 percent of admitted first-year students: 30–33
Note: You should check a school's website to determine whether it superscores (that is, takes applicants' highest sectional scores from multiple test administrations and sums them for a composite score) and if it has a test-optional policy. If the school does not require students to submit test scores, find out what percentage of students did not send in scores last year and whether their grade point average or other academic criteria varied from those who did submit scores.

While some schools will publish an exact average, many use a range or "middle 50 percent" numbers. Students often misinterpret those numbers and think either the low-end number is a minimum or the top-end number is a guarantee of admission. Remember that these are middle 50 percent scores, so 25 percent of the admitted class scored above or below each number.

4.12

Balance the Buckets

On the buckets below, write the names of the colleges on your list where they fit; try to strike a balance across the three.

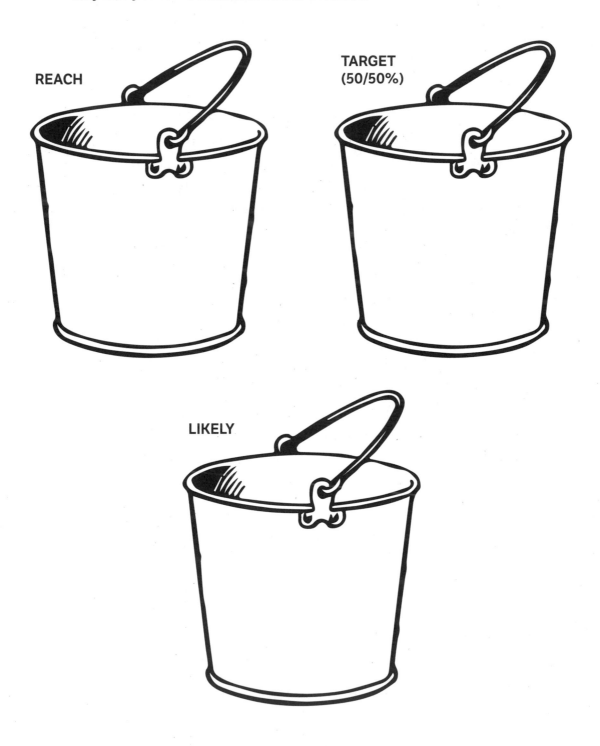

4.13

Admission Plans

You will find a growing number of ways that colleges structure their admission process. Some offer several different options, and others only provide one or two different plans and deadlines. It can be hard to keep them all straight, and you must determine which is the best for you. Use this table to understand each option, and consider the questions that follow about which one might be appropriate for you.

ADMISSION PLAN	DESCRIPTION	DEADLINE FOR FALL ENTRY	NOTES
Rolling admission	Students may apply at any time after the application period opens. Admission offers are made on a rolling basis until all spots are filled, at which time most schools will still accept applications for the waitlist.	Late summer or early fall. Ongoing.	Often found at schools using formulaic admission. Some schools may fill their entering class early, so don't delay unless you are waiting on testing or another semester to show improved academic achievement.
Early decision (ED) I and II	A binding agreement by which a student can apply to only one school, where they will commit to enrolling if admitted.	ED I: usually 10/15, 11/1, 11/15, or 12/1. ED II: usually 1/1 or 1/15.	You should apply only if you are certain that the school is the best match for you. Colleges often accept recruited athletes and other niche priorities through these plans. Check admit rate differentials between ED and RD at schools you consider.
Early action (EA) I and II	A *nonbinding* agreement with an early deadline.	EA I: usually 10/15, 11/1, 11/15, or 12/1. EA II: usually 1/1 or 1/15.	While this plan varies from school to school, there is often a benefit of applying EA because it is nonbinding and you get a decision earlier. Check the admit rate differential between EA and RD at colleges you are considering.
Restrictive early action / Single-choice early action	A hybrid plan where students can apply and receive decisions early under a nonbinding agreement, but in doing so they agree not to apply to another school under an ED plan.	Usually 10/15, 11/1, 11/15, or 12/1.	Be sure to read the policy on the admission website to understand restrictions and requirements.
Regular decision (RD)	Standard admission application.	Usually in early January or February with notification in late March.	This is the most common way students apply to college.
Priority applicationsw	This term often refers to an earlier deadline by which a student must apply to be considered in the school's first round of review.	Usually 11/30 or 12/1.	This plan is rare, but it is important to learn if a college (typically a larger state system) has it.

Consider these questions as you decide when and how to apply:

Is there one school that you would attend regardless of where else you were accepted?

Will financial aid be a determining factor in your decision of where to attend?

Will grades or test scores from your senior fall or winter strengthen your application?

Are there reasons you should not submit an application in the fall?

Which application plan is most appealing to you and why?

Which application plan is best for you at the various colleges you are considering?

4.14

Family Forward

Every year at the holidays my (Brennan's) kids make a Christmas gift wish list. When they were little, they would rifle through the department store flyers and circle the shiny toys and gadgets of which they dreamed. As a sign of the times and their adolescence, they now share a Google doc with me each year with hyperlinks to the items on their list. So much for the magic of Santa's workshop; these days, they might as well be writing to Amazon. Their lists have also gotten more realistic as they have matured, though there are almost always one or two big-ticket wishes among the balance of clothes, posters, and other reasonable requests. They know that they will not receive everything on the list, and often they have listed items in order of interest. Don't worry; they are not completely devoid of holiday spirit; thankfully, they are equally excited about getting and giving to others. It sure does make my shopping life easier, though!

Parents: Over the next few months, your student is going to be making lists and checking them much more than twice. We have encouraged your student to revisit, refine, and rework their list, so know that changes are good. It means they are closely considering what they want in a college. They might initially go for the shiny schools that everyone is talking about. They might be dreaming big, or they might take a more balanced approach. How you respond to them along the way is going to make all the difference. Your job is to be patient and to withhold judgment. To listen. Your job is not to make their list for them, just like it would be a fool's errand for me to write up a Christmas list for my kids. However, as we talked about in chapter 3, proactive communication about expectations and limitations, when approached with empathy, care, and clarity, will make discussion around their list more productive and unified.

The bottom line (even if it does not always come across this way) is they want your input; they value your opinion; and they need your guidance and support. As in so many aspects of parenting, your challenge is to figure out when and how to do that.

We have asked your student to engage with a lot of exercises in this chapter as they get excited about the colleges they might consider. We are now going to ask you to do the same and then come together with your student at the end of the chapter to compare notes.

4.15

Family Word Choice

Please circle the words or phrases below that best represent what you think will be important to your student in a college or university, underline those that are important to you, and cross out those words and phrases that do not apply. You do not need to circle, underline, or cross out every item. Leaving a factor untouched simply indicates that neither you nor your student feels strongly about it.

Academic support	Coed school
Close to home	Cutting-edge academics
Urban	Socially conservative
Intramural sports	Famous for science
Famous professors	Intense
Competitive students	Accessible professors
Personal	Campus life
Cold	Graduate programs
Large classes	School spirit
Cosmopolitan	Friendly
Few requirements	Research oriented
Many international students	Small classes
Core curriculum	Classes taught by professors
Religious atmosphere	Intellectual
Unconventional students	Single-sex school

Leadership opportunities	Subdued social life
Many outdoor activities	Athletics are important
Rural	Strong study abroad
Many cultural activities	Warm
Ethnically diverse student body	Safe
Fraternities and sororities	Liberal arts
Everyone knows you	Admission test optional
Dress-conscious students	Preprofessional programs
Ivy League	Student activism
Active in arts and music	Transportation
Personal atmosphere	Reasonable cost

What factors are missing? Add your own words or phrases to this list, and revisit this exercise as your family receives brochures and emails from schools, visits campuses, and gets ready to apply to college.

4.16

Family Free Association

When you build a college list, first write down the schools you know about or have visited in the past. Doing this will help you identify any preconceived notions or past experiences of yours that might influence your views. In the table below, write down colleges that come to mind and note how you are familiar with them (for example, you or someone you know attended, sports team, a drive through campus, other parents talk about it). In the final column, write the first three words that come to mind when you think of this college. Don't overthink it. Just list your initial thoughts.

Name of college	How do you know it?	Three descriptive words

Once you are done, take some time to discuss these schools and your perceptions with a friend or colleague. See if they agree with your impressions of the schools or have additional information or opinions that may lead you to ask more questions or investigate further. Later in this chapter we will ask you to do this again in the Come Together section.

4.17

Family Rankings

On a daily basis, we are inundated with numbers. Whether it be sports statistics, stock fluctuations, or miles per gallon, quantifiable comparisons fill our television screens and newsfeeds. Rankings and ratings are also incredibly prevalent. While these can be helpful to consider, before you believe any numbers, percentages, or relative assigned values, and certainly before you use them to make personal decisions or form an opinion, it is important to know their source, how they were developed and formulated, and the motives of their source.

Unfortunately, we have found that too often parents take college rankings and ratings at face value and draw arbitrary or hard lines without considering how they were was created. Take college rankings. You will find a ridiculous number and variety of these online—from who has the most benches to the best ice cream to the coolest faculty members. Just promise us that before you put too much stock in any of these, you will look at the methodology behind their creation and ask if those metrics really matter to you and your student.

Every year students tell us they were pressured only to apply, or ultimately to select, colleges ranked at or above a certain threshold. In our experience, that type of mentality severely limits a productive and comprehensive college search. Instead, our sincere hope is that you will be invested and confident enough to examine closely what really matters to you and your family.

Earlier in this chapter, we asked your student to create a ranking system for colleges based on their own criteria. Now it is your turn. Use the table below to list the factors that are important to you as you think about your student's college search. Then, for each factor, give the colleges a rating from *1 = not impressed* to *10 = nearly ideal*. At the end, you can total your ratings if you wish, but the most important part is that you know why you assigned these ratings and how you weighted each factor. Some examples of factors you might rate are *faculty accessibility, safety, housing, internships, academic major.*

College	Criteria #1	Criteria #2	Criteria #3	Criteria #4	Criteria #5	Criteria #6	Criteria #7	Criteria #8	Criteria #9	Total score

───────────── **4.18** ─────────────

Come Together

This chapter has been filled with hands-on exercises to help students develop their college list with their parents' support. Don't attempt it all in one sitting, and definitely take a break before you debrief as a family. These will be ongoing conversations as you research, visit, revisit, and apply, and your list will both expand and shrink throughout the admission experience.

Initial Influences

Students: To begin, share your responses from exercises 4.1 Influencer Impact and 4.2 Resources Reliability about the resources you will use and the people who will influence your list development.

Parents: Do you have anything to add or observations to make about factors your student may not have considered?

Common Exercises

Everyone: Compare your responses to the Word Choice exercises (4.3 and 4.15). What words did you circle or cross out in common? Where did you differ? Were you surprised by factors that are important to the student but not family or vice versa? Do the same with the exercise Free Association (4.6 and 4.16). Did you list any of the same schools? If so, were the words you thought of to describe the schools similar or different? Where did you hear about different schools? What stands out to you about the schools on each other's lists and how they are described?

Interest, Needs, and Criteria

Students: Share your Mind Map (4.7), Needs and Wants (4.4), and your Criteria Grid (4.5) exercises with your family. Why did you choose to map the interests you did? Expand on why you categorized the school factors the way you did, and discuss your growing understanding of the criteria you are using to build your list. What was a challenge for you as you worked through these exercises? What was obvious to you immediately?

Parents: Would you have chosen the same interests for them to map? What would you add or suggest about the career choices they identified as related to their interests? What surprises you about the school criteria your student identified? Is there anything you think they left out? If not, what would you have mapped?

Rankings

Everyone: Discuss the role and importance of commercial college rankings like those of *U.S. News and World Report*. What stands out about the criteria the company uses to create them? Compare your responses to the ranking exercises (4.10, 4.11, and 4.17). What criteria did you choose for your personal ranking? Were any of them the same; if so, did you rate them similarly for the colleges you listed in common? What surprised you about how each of you ranked schools?

Financial Fit

Students: Share your completed financial fit worksheet. Together, discuss how you will approach your college list development over the coming months and how the reality of costs, loans, and return on investment will influence the list.

Funnels and Buckets

Students: Share your funnel diagram (4.8) with your family. Show them the schools you listed in the widest tier at top, and talk them through how you will narrow the set of schools during your search. Show your family the balanced buckets (4.12) with your prospective colleges sorted into categories based on their selectivity and your scholastic record. Return to these exercises during your regular family meetings to check in on how your search is developing.

Parents: Would you add any schools to the funnel? Are there any that you have concerns about? Do you think your student has the right schools in the right buckets? If not, share your thoughts.

Final Thoughts

This is a lot of work to do, and it can lead to some tension, disagreement, or even hurt feelings and bruised egos. Make sure you are checking in on the emotional responses you are having to each other's reactions, comments, and concerns, and don't just concentrate on the business of list building. Trust us: putting in this kind of work now, having critical conversations early on, and deciding what really matters to you is what allows you to move forward honestly, openly, and jointly. Hopefully, working together is also starting to help you laugh and enjoy the shared experience. If that is not the case, pause the meeting, put down the book, and go do something together that you all enjoy. College is important. But family is really what this is all about.

Chapter 5

The College Visit

The exercises in chapter 4 were designed to help you identify a list of schools that line up with the experience you want to have in college. As a result, our hope is that you have narrowed the *funnel* (see 4.8) of places you are considering, while continuing to stay open to discovering new schools. If that is the case, you are on the right track. Now it is time to take your list for a test drive by visiting colleges.

A great place to start is by doing a deep dive into a college's website beyond the webinars and interactive tools hosted by the admission office. Interested in intramural sports, study abroad, or robotics? Check out the college's social media channels. Unlike the college itself, or the admission and financial aid offices, these channels are not marketing to you. That means the content is authentic, organic, and representative of the true student experience. Look at the latest student newspaper and alumni magazine online and pay attention to the issues, problems, points of pride, and things the college is raising money for or building on campus. Again, these are signs of priorities and focus areas that will help you understand what you can likely expect in your time on campus. Email faculty or students, and use LinkedIn or other networks to connect with current students or alumni you might know to learn about their experience. These are all easy and free ways to determine whether you want to take the time to visit campus.

We understand you may not have the time, ability, or resources to travel to all the campuses on your list, and that is totally fine. One of the best things you can do initially is visit campuses that are close to home to see what resonates with you. It is likely that in your state or city you have a variety of public and private schools that range in size, setting, and campus feel. Just walking around and getting a sense of different schools, even if you do not set up an official tour or information session with the admission office, is a great first step.

Online sessions and virtual tours are another free and easy way to both expand and narrow your college choices. While the COVID-19 pandemic was devastating, one of the silver linings is that it radically increased the offerings and improved the quality of virtual opportunities colleges offer. Your access to current students, admission officers, faculty members, as well as live and recorded information sessions and virtual tours, is far greater than it was pre-pandemic.

If you are able to set aside the time and money, you and your family or friends may be able to go on a college tour to visit a number of campuses in a multiday trip. If you are on campus, we hope you will build in time beyond the tour and information session. Remember that everything "official" is going to be polished, spun, and marketed to impress you. Get off the beaten path and explore campus on your own. Go to the places where you think you would spend time based on your major or interests. Loiter appropriately. Grab lunch and sit on the quad or in the dining hall, and just listen and watch. Walk off campus too. See what the surrounding area feels like, and think how you might engage with that city or town as a student, because this is an element of campus tours too frequently omitted.

Regardless of precisely how and when you visit schools, your job is to ensure you are leaving time to process what you are experiencing and taking notes along the way about your thoughts, opinions, and reactions. In this chapter, we will walk you through ways to visit, provide you with questions to ask, and give you prompts to consider as you interact with campus community members and dig deeper into the culture and dynamics of the colleges on your list.

We have seen students eliminate colleges because the weather was bad the day they visited or the tour guide (one out of fifteen thousand students on campus) wore a shirt they did not like. We think there is a better way. Our goal in the activities ahead is to help you make the most of your visits and interactions with students, staff, and faculty members, ask the questions that truly matter to you, and ultimately use common criteria to figure out which places should stay on your list and which ones you can drop.

5.1

Know Your Role

The college search experience is one of transition. It asks families to begin shifting who is in the driver's seat. Before you begin to schedule college visits, determine the role you and your family members will each play in the planning, visit, and follow-up. It is best to discuss this ahead of the visit. Add your own roles and responsibilities to the table.

ROLE	STUDENT	PARENT/ SUPPORTER	BOTH
Schedule tours and info session			
Set up interview (if applicable)			
Plan visit (hotel, meals, etc.)			
Ask questions during visit			
Talk with financial aid office			
Meet with a coach or professor			
Take notes			

5.2

Question Your Questions

"Be Prepared!" There is a reason this is the Boy Scout motto: when you head out into the wilderness, you must think ahead and be ready for anything. As you venture out to explore colleges, the same holds true. While you can show up to a campus and simply accept what the people there are selling, your visit will be much more meaningful and informative if you arrive knowing the questions that matter the most to you and refuse to accept superficial answers.

Think back on what you listed as your needs and wants (4.4). Then check out our examples below and formulate questions that get to the heart of what you are trying to understand.

What you want to know	Superficial question	Pointed question
Accessibility of faculty and classroom experience	What is the faculty-to-student ratio?	What is your typical introductory class size? How does class size vary from first year to senior year? Is the range higher or lower for the major(s) that I am considering?
Do most students graduate in four or six years?	What's your graduation rate?	How does the graduation rate vary by major? What percentage of students who double major, study abroad, conduct research, or have an internship finish in four years?
Are students happy at the school and stay after the first year?	What is your first-year retention rate?	Why do students leave? Is it related to finances? Are the students who leave disproportionately in certain majors or from out of state? What resources are on campus for supporting students academically?

5.3

Campus Visit Checklist

Develop a list of questions that you want answered at each school about academic majors and programs, as well as life outside the classroom. Some areas to ask about might be internships, career counseling, housing options, freshman retention, social life, safety, or travel abroad. (But don't ask, "How is your biology department?" You will invariably get "Oh, it's great!")

☐ Connect with the admission dean who is responsible for your high school or the area where you live. If that individual is not available, ask for their contact information or business card.

☐ Allow ample time to wander campus and grab a coffee or meal after you leave the admission office.

☐ Ask at the admission office if you can have lunch in the dining hall or for a popular off-campus recommendation.

☐ Find a random student (non–tour guide) and ask their thoughts on the college, accessibility of professors, school spirit, support structures (tutoring, writing center, career resources, etc.) and what it is like to live in the area.

☐ Stop by the academic department you have an interest in and talk with a professor and/or student.

☐ Ideally, contact the department beforehand to see if you can meet with someone. Ask about the department's research or other special programs. Even if you cannot meet with someone in the department, see if you can find examples of student work or projects on display.

☐ Contact a coach, music director, etc. beforehand to set up a meeting during your campus visit. Better yet, attend an athletic event or concert or other production. This will let you observe school spirit and support for student endeavors.

☐ Pick up the student newspaper. You will find that it generally offers an uncensored take on campus issues.

☐ At the end of your visits, ask yourself what story each college was trying to tell through the tour and information session. Make notes immediately so that you don't lose a record of your initial impressions.

5.4

You Are Here

Whether you are visiting a college in person or virtually, it is important to get a sense of place. After all, this will be your home for at least the next four years, and how comfortable you are in your surroundings will go a long way toward allowing you to feel safe, enjoy your experience, and succeed. Try the following approaches to get to know campus and beyond.

In-person probing

Get Lost: Want to get a good sense for how welcoming a campus is? Try standing in the middle of a quad or another busy place on campus when classes are letting out. Look as lost as possible. Maybe take out a campus map and point at it with a perplexed look on your face. See how long it takes for someone to stop and offer you assistance.

Eat Up: Grab a meal in a campus dining hall. Not only will you be able to size up the quality of the food, but you'll also get to observe and eavesdrop on student interactions.

Supermarket Sweep: One can tell a lot about an area by going into the neighborhood supermarket and checking out the offerings and also the people who live in the community. Take some time to stop by a local grocery store, and pick up a few items and some intel.

Coffee Chat: On your way in or out of town, stop at an off-campus café for a drink. Ideally you would hang out for a while and observe the comings and goings, but at the very least, get in line to purchase your beverage and chat up the other patrons and barista about the local area and their impressions of the college and its students. Are "town and gown" relations healthy or strained and how and why?

Chamber Check: Stop by the local Chamber of Commerce or information kiosk if there is one. How is the area marketed? What events, activities, community organizations, etc., exist?

News Brief: Pick up the local newspaper or magazine to get a better sense of the community. If you are staying in the area overnight, watch the local news, or if you're just passing through, tune in to the local radio station. Ideally, do all three of these, and see what common themes emerge.

Virtual vetting

Pin Drop: Although there is no substitute for stepping foot on campus for that gut feeling, all is not lost if finances, schedule, or even a pandemic prevent you from doing so. In addition to the formal online campus tour, zoom in on Google Earth for a better look around. Drop a pin on different locations on campus, and try out the real-time street view. Check out what is going on. Do this on different days, at various times, and, if possible, in multiple seasons.

Read and Listen Up: Access the student paper, local paper, regional Patch, police blog, etc. to see what is going on. Search using the name of the college and town online to see what stories pop up. Listen to livestreams of local radio stations or watch the local news.

Get Some Yelp: Undeniably, Yelp and other reviews are subjective, but by searching for local businesses, restaurants, and attractions, you can get a feeling for how the masses (or at least trolls) view what the area has to offer.

Be Social: Search Facebook, Instagram, LinkedIn, and other social media sites for official and informal groups in the area. Follow them or just check in from time to time to see what is happening in the community.

Lessons Learned

Whether you visited campus and community in person, virtually, or both (ideally), consider the following questions:

What if anything had you heard about the college and area before you started exploring?

Did your visit confirm what you had heard or change your opinion?

What surprised you about the campus?

What surprised you about the town?

Are there other thoughts, notes, impressions, answers you need?

5.5

Scavenger Hunt

Is your brain going to explode if one more time you hear how many books are held in a college's library or you endure another explanation of the blue safety-light system common on most campuses?

Designing your personalized scavenger hunt will keep you alert, add creativity to make your visits more memorable, allow you to dig deeper into a college community, and provide an innovative way to contrast different schools. We hope you will include items or challenges on your hunt that are geared toward your specific interests, but we have provided two suggestions to get you started. Check the item or challenge off as you accomplish it. Share your scavenger hunt idea with a friend or classmate to see if they have ideas of other things to include.

CHALLENGE	CHECK OFF	COMMENTS
Collect a student newspaper.		
Ask about the college's most famous student tradition.		

5.6

Admission Bingo

Most colleges and universities have developed extensive virtual admission programs, including tours, open houses, high school visits, interviews, and information sessions. Some are recorded and can be viewed anytime. Others are live events in either webinar form, where participants can type in questions during the presentation, or a video-meeting format where participants can interact directly with the admission staff. You can use a fun bingo game during these virtual events or for in-person presentations (be subtle) on college campuses, at your high school, or in your area.

Each row in the grid has one square in which can write your own topic or question. Be sure to get answers before you leave the session.

Famous alumni	Total number of undergraduate students .	Your question	First-year housing options or requirements
Your question	Name of the school's mascot	Is this school test-optional? YES NO	What is the first-year retention rate?
Does this school use a holistic review process? YES NO	Average class size	What admission plans are available for first-year admission?	Your question
Name of a campus tradition	What is the four-year graduation rate?	Your question	First-year class size or admit rate

5.7

Variety of Voices

If you are looking to buy a car, would you ask only the dealer for an opinion? More likely you would seek a number of perspectives and look for consistency across answers to determine what is objective and what subjective. This is your job in the college selection process too. Take the time to ask *as many people as possible your questions*. This will help you see the big picture and get a true sense of campus culture.

Use the form below to ensure you are getting a variety of views about the colleges you are considering. Are the perspectives similar, or are they variable? We have suggested a few questions to get you started.

Question	Student	Admission officer	Tour guide	Professor	Alum	
What is the most exciting thing happening on campus?						
What makes this college different from other schools?						
How does this college set students up for success and fulfillment in the future?						

5.8

Tour Topics

The following is a list of questions you might ask a campus tour guide:

- How many people are in most of your classes? What was the largest/ smallest class you have taken?

- Who teaches you in these classes? Professors mainly? Grad students?

- Does this college have a core curriculum of classes I will need to take before getting into my major?

- When do you have to declare your major? What are the most popular majors? Are there majors being eliminated?

- Tell me about housing for first-year students? Where did you live, and what did you like and not like about it? Do many students live off campus? If so, where and why?

- Do students seem to study primarily to earn good grades? Are students competitive with one another or more collaborative? What is the attitude toward working hard?

- How available are your professors to meet one on one with students? Have you gotten to know any faculty outside class?

- Can you tell me anything firsthand about the department of (French, English, history, [your intended major])?

- What's the biggest issue in local campus politics?

- Are students aware of and active about big issues in national or international politics?

- What percentage of students study abroad at some time while in college?

- What impact does Greek life have here? Athletics?

- What are weekends like?

- How active is student government? What activities are popular?

- Are the arts supported here? Are the courses oversubscribed? Which academic areas are strong?

- What do you think is the greatest shortcoming of this college? What do students complain about?

- What do you like best about your experience and education here?

5.9

Campus Closeout

After each college visit, create a document with headings like the one below.

Name of college:

Visit date:

Who, if anyone, accompanied you?

Interviewer:

Tour guide:

Other individuals you met:

More information you wish to gather:

Key impressions/features of the college:

Pros:

Cons:

Final Assessment:

Rate on a scale of 0 to 5 (0 = not interested; 5 = loved it):

5.10

Family Forward

No matter your career, whether you like it or not, you are also a gig worker. Like a chauffeur, taxi driver, or Uber/Lyft hack, you have spent more than a decade and a half helping your student get around. From school to friends' houses, sports practices, and myriad other activities, you do it because you love them and want them to have opportunities. These car rides offered different experiences over the years. Those painful hours spent listening incessantly to children's music morphed into eavesdropping on preteen conversations about who liked whom or seemingly all-important events of the day. As full teenager mode kicked in, you probably had to bite your tongue to resist asking questions that would have resulted in shrugs or one-word answers anyway. Good news: you will get to put all of that training to use now.

College visits present a great opportunity not just to spend time with your student but also to grow closer while you are learning and exploring together. More importantly, visits let a student get a better feeling for a campus community and its offerings. We hope you will see your job primarily as a good partner on these trips who finds appropriate moments to weigh in, offer helpful insights, and ask questions that are supportive rather than overbearing. Of course, you will form your own opinions on the schools you visit, but all that tongue-biting practice is now to be put to good use. Naturally, you will also have your own questions about each school, but be judicious in your inquiries and comments. We are not saying you don't or won't get to offer input on the planning and execution of your student's visits, but be willing to defer and let them own it, and define your role as they see best.

While time, schedules, or resources may not allow for an in-person experience of each college, the proliferation of virtual tours and programming provides a great window into colleges. At times, we hope you can find the opportunity to "attend" these as a family so that you can learn, listen, and debrief your impressions together.

Soon your student will be off to college, and though you will have more free time, you will secretly miss the hours spent with them in the car as a captive audience. Take advantage of these fleeting moments. And one final tip: do not buy college gear in your size on one of your campus visits, as this is a dead giveaway of your preferences.

━━━━━━━━━━━━━━ **5.11** ━━━━━━━━━━━━━━

Aid Analysis

Whether you are going to tour a campus, participate in a virtual event, or reach out via email, here are some questions you can ask or look into online to get an idea of what financial aid opportunities look like at a school. Our friend and colleague Diane Campbell, director of college counseling at Liberty Common High School in Fort Collins, Colorado, encourages parents to ask a version of these questions.

1. What does the typical financial aid award look like for first-year students?

Most students attending four-year colleges qualify for some financial aid, but the type and mix vary depending on a college's policies and priorities.

A financial aid award can be made up of a combination of grants, scholarships, loans, and work- study opportunities. Keep in mind that while grants and scholarships do not need to be paid back, loans do. If a college promises in its promotional materials to meet 100 percent of a student's need, it's important to know how the college plans to do that.

Also ask

How much need are you meeting?

And how does that break out into loans, work, grants, and scholarships?

2. What kinds of scholarships are available to students?

A campus visit can be a good time to find out whether a school awards financial aid for characteristics other than need, such as institutional priorities, for instance. (We cover this topic in chapter 8.) This is often be referred to as "merit aid" or "scholarship aid."

Also ask

How are scholarships awarded, and are they renewable after the first year? Often colleges provide a one-year grant or scholarship that is not renewable, so it is extremely important to understand both the amount and time frame.

Is there scholarship money earmarked for geography, gender, major, high school, specific companies, or military families?

3. How long does it take the typical student to graduate?

This question obviously has significant financial implications. If a school's average years to graduation is a concern, it's important to drill down and find out the cause.

Also ask

Do graduation rates vary by major because of the number of course requirements?

Is there a lack of course availability or student support causing lower graduation rates?

Is financial aid at your college restricted to a specific number of semesters?

4. How much on average do students end up borrowing?

Universities are required to track and report the total amount in federal loans that their graduates borrowed.

Also ask

What is the average annual loan amount for your students? And does that amount vary from first year to fourth year?

What is the average starting salary of your graduates? And do you have job placement rates by major?

5. Do you grant course credit for passing Advanced Placement exams and for dual enrollment?

You want to know whether any course credits or test scores you bring with you could be awarded credit and therefore reduce your costs.

Also ask

What minimum score or grade is required for credit?

6. Do you stack scholarships?

It is very important to know if a college allows you to add any outside scholarships you have to the aid the college awards you (that is, to "stack" scholarships) or if it reduces its own aid by the amount of the outside money you receive.

Also ask

Are scholarships linked to GPA, test scores, both, or can you tell me other factors used to allot scholarships?

Can you recommend good websites or other resources for finding more opportunities for outside scholarships?

7. What am I not asking that I should be about financial aid and scholarships?

5.12

Come Together

Ideally, your college visits will bring you closer as a family and create some memories that will last long beyond your college years. The Know Your Role exercise (5.1) is an important place to start, and we suggest that, before your first campus visit, review all the exercises in this chapter as a family to create and agree on a game plan.

- Look over the Tour Topics (5.8) and decide what questions you want to ask and who will ask them (hint: it should be the student).

- Discuss the Question Your Questions exercise (5.2) to develop questions that will go below the surface.

- Generate your own Scavenger Hunt list using the example in activity 5.5.

- Determine what various campus voices you want to hear during your visit, and write them down in the worksheet in 5.7.

After each visit, both student and parent can fill out the Campus Closeout debrief form in section 5.9, and once you have visited one or two campuses, use your regular family college meeting to compare notes and talk about how they went. Let questions like these guide your conversation:

What were the highlights of your visits?

What was most helpful?

What did you miss while there?

What would you do differently?

Part III

Chapter 6

Admission Factors I

WHAT ARE COLLEGES LOOKING FOR ACADEMICALLY?

Up to this point, we have largely focused on you and your family. *Why do you want to go to college? What are your goals, dreams, hopes, and interests? What is truly important to you and your family as you visit, apply to, and select a school?*

Now we are going to shift our attention to the colleges themselves. Our hope is you have begun to gain a sense of how vast the landscape of American higher education is. Although colleges may send you brochures that all seem to have the same pictures—happy students strolling across manicured lawns, kids in lab coats examining colored liquids in beakers, and professors passionately lecturing in front of classrooms of enthralled students—the truth is that the location, size, academic focus, campus culture, and general feel of each place is unique.

It stands to reason then that colleges do not all make admission decisions the same way. In this chapter we will help you understand generally what colleges are looking for from an academic standpoint, how you can learn more about the admission process of each school you are considering, and how to put your best foot forward with your application.

Essentially, there are two ways that schools make admission decisions—formulaic (numbers based) and holistic (the numbers and more) review.

Formulaic Admission Review

If a college utilizes formulaic review, you are going to know it. The numbers that govern admission will be all over its website (often including an online calculator or chart to plug in your scores and grades) and in its publications. And the college's representatives will spend time describing these calculations in admission presentations, at college fairs, or in your high school.

The good news is that you essentially know before you apply whether you will be admitted. Formulaic review is largely black and white, plain and simple, cut and dried. Found almost exclusively at public colleges and universities, formulaic review is like running the hurdles in a track meet. These schools adjust their bar to varying heights based on grade point average (GPA) and test scores. Admission is determined by whether you clear the bar or fall short. The theory is that any student who has the grades and scores to clear it can be academically successful on campus, and importantly, the college has the room in its classes, residence halls, and student center to accommodate anyone who meets these thresholds.

Holistic Admission Review

If formulaic admission is like running the hurdles, holistic review is like competing in the decathlon or the all-around events in gymnastics in that multiple factors with slight differentiations are humanly judged.

The good news is that you will not be evaluated solely on your grades or test scores. More good news: people have empathy and consider context. The bad news is that holistic review is gray rather than black and white, and the judges are evaluating multiple factors beyond academics because of the strength of their applicant pool. Therefore, it will be difficult, and in some cases impossible, to predict whether you will be admitted.

If a college you are considering uses holistic review, it is doing so because it receives more applications from academically qualified students than it has space available in the entering class. Additionally, the college is signaling that, beyond merely the academic ability to succeed in the classroom, it wants to enroll students who will enhance the campus community as students and alumni. From a practical standpoint, this also means that its application is more involved than those for colleges with formulaic review, but we will get to all of that in the coming chapters.

Context is everything for colleges with holistic review. This means that when admission readers analyze your transcript, they do not simply take the weighted or unweighted GPA at face value. Instead, they will be asking lots of questions and digging deeper. Admission readers will consider your grades from each year in high school and look for any evident trends. They will evaluate your school's academic profile to understand which courses you had access to and will consider the grading scale you were evaluated with as well. In other words, those humans are going to be asking specific, detailed questions in order to understand your academic context: *What courses did you have access to in high school? What could you have taken each year? What did you choose to take? And how did you do in each class, school year, and subject area.*

Clearly, they have a lot of questions. You likely do as well. Let's help you start finding some answers.

6.1

Profile Preview

Take a look at your high school's profile. Usually you can find this pretty quickly on your school's website or in the counseling office. In this document, you will normally find a list of courses by subject, your school's grading scale, and other academically related information about whether your school weights GPAs and which courses are required for graduation. A profile provides critical information for admission counselors, and it is frequently where they begin their review to understand your particular school, options, and context.

As a student, this may be the first time you have seen your school's profile. What stands out to you? Did you learn anything after reviewing it? What is most prominently featured?

If you were a college admission counselor reviewing this profile, what are your immediate impressions or takeaways about your school?

Knowing that admission readers are looking for your grading scale, courses offered, and any weighting your school may use in calculating grades, do you find that information readily?

Knowing your school, do you find any information missing from its profile that you think is important? If so, note that here. (This information may be helpful if you have to fill in any gaps in your academic record when you complete your applications or have interviews for admission or scholarships.)

Bonus: To get an idea of what it is like to be an admission officer, go look at the profile for another high school in your area. What stands out to you about the profile?

How does this profile differ from your school's profile?

What does this profile feature?

6.2

Transcript Takeaways

Go online and download your unofficial transcript or request one from your school.

Once you have it, record your current cumulative GPA here: _____
(If your school does not provide a GPA, you can use an online calculator to determine a ballpark GPA. See https://gpacalculator.net/high-school-gpa-calculator/.)

Some high schools include a weighted and unweighted GPA or an academic GPA and cumulative GPA. If you have a second GPA, record it here: _____

If you are applying to a college using formulaic review, this is typically as far as the readers will go in delving into your transcript, although some will perform their own GPA recalculations.

Depending on your current year in school, record your GPA from each grade individually.

ninh _____

tenth _____

eleventh _____

Tracking Trends

In addition to reviewing your overall GPA and evaluating and rating the rigor of your curriculum (covered in 6.3), many schools will also look subject by subject and grade by grade. They are attempting to determine if you have been consistent, have improved, or have declined over time and if you typically perform better in certain subject areas versus others.

Now, to answer the questions below, we want you to pretend you are an admission counselor in a college that uses holistic review. (Feel free to snack on, listen to, or wear whatever you think admission counselors would while doing this if it helps you get in character.)

1. Circle the option that describes your grade trend since the ninth grade:

    A. Escalating and Improving

    B. Consistent

    C. Declining

    D. Varied and Inconsistent

2. As an admission counselor, what patterns do you see or observations can you make about your overall performance in each of these subject areas: math, English, social science and history, science, foreign language, others/electives.

3. Does the rigor of your courses vary by subject area? If so, make notes on that here (and keep this in mind as you consider particular colleges and majors).

6.3

Rating Rigor

To rate the extent to which you challenged yourself in high school, some colleges will count and record the number of "rigorous" courses (Advanced Placement, International Baccalaureate, honors, dual enrollment, or advanced) you took. Most institutions using holistic review, however, have developed an internal rubric to rate the strength of your curriculum choices based on the curriculum available in your school's profile. Review the example rubric below.

Rating	Description
5	Extremely challenging course selection in all subject areas. May have gone beyond high school offerings to seek additional courses.
4	Highly challenging course selection in all subject areas.
3	Moderately challenging course selection in most subject areas.
2	Less challenging course selection in some or most subject areas.
1	No evidence of rigorous course selection.
Notes	

Note: In most admission offices, after the initial review of a transcript, at least one or two other staff members will read notes and review transcripts.

Based on your course choices since ninth grade, circle the rating in the rubric (5–1) that characterizes the rigor of your curriculum overall and make brief notes as a counselor would about your evaluation.

If you are comfortable doing it, ask a friend to switch transcripts with you and walk through the questions and prompts in exercises 6.2 and 6.3. You can learn a great deal from additional perspectives and observations.

Did your friend have a similar assessment of your grade trend and rigor of curriculum?

Does that align with your evaluation? (*Note*: It is common for admission counselors to disagree. When that is the case, they will add notes to your file for additional layers of review or committee evaluation.)

Does your friend's evaluation of your choices in certain years or subject areas vary from their overall rating?

Ask them to make any additional comments on your academic choices, performance, and rigor of curriculum.

What takeaways or comments do they provide that are helpful to you in understanding how colleges may read the academic portion of your application?

6.4
Testing Takes

Op-eds, books, and documentaries have criticized, supported, unraveled, and unpacked standardized testing. Research (and research about the research) and criticism are to be expected when testing generates millions of dollars each year from the administration of the SAT and ACT, test prep, and state contracts. Bottom line: it's complicated.

There was a time when some colleges accepted only one test or the other, or strongly recommended one. This is no longer true, yet students often find they prefer the SAT or ACT because of format, pace, content, or perhaps a practical issue such as where and when a particular test is offered.

ACT or SAT

This exercise is designed to help you understand how the ACT and SAT are similar and different so that you can plan your approach to standardized testing. Go to act.org and collegeboard.org and find descriptions of the different test sections and the subject matter they cover. Find information about test administration as well. Use the table below to compare the tests.

Website	www.collegeboard.com	www.act.org
Cost of test		
Upcoming administration dates		
Testing site nearby		
Length of test (in minutes) and total number of questions		
Score range and national average		
Names of sections		
Number of questions per section		

Website	www.collegeboard.com	www.act.org
Content covered in sections		
Criteria for waiving the fee required to take the test		
Notes and observations		

Is your high school a test administration site? If not, where is the closest one to you?

Based on the criteria listed, are you eligible for a fee waiver for either test? If so, contact your school counselor.

Take time to create an account on the website of the ACT, College Board, or both and access more information about the tests, including instructional videos, sample questions and practice tests, and other tips and strategies for test taking.

Examine the differences between the two tests by finding articles online that compare and contrast them.

Seek out *concordance tables* online to understand equivalent scores for the two tests. For instance, if you score 29 on the ACT, what is the equivalent score on the SAT?

Talk to your guidance counselor and at least one older student about their experiences and recommendations.

Listen

Mark Stucker, a college counselor at KIPP schools in Atlanta, an independent counselor, and a former colleague of mine (Brennan), interviewed Applerouth Tutoring's CEO and founder, Dr. Jed Applerouth, on the *Your College-Bound Kid* podcast (https://yourcollegeboundkid.com/2018/08/). They covered important topics about the SAT and ACT.

Check out episode 28 at the 39:40 mark:

- How is the ACT different from the SAT?

- How can you determine which test to take?

- How can you start preparing for the test?

In episode 29, they continue the conversation on testing at the 31:10 mark:

- What do you do when you are running out of time when taking the SAT or ACT?

- Do you need to know science to do well on the ACT?

- How do the essay portions of the SAT and ACT differ?

- How do you give a student confidence for taking the SAT or ACT?

- *Note: Episode 29 also addresses the seven factors that admission officers like to see in a student.*

6.5

Test Optional

Over the past few decades, and particularly with the coming of the COVID-19 pandemic, many colleges have determined that standardized testing is not an essential component in their admission review process. When applying to these *test-optional* colleges, you can choose whether or not to submit standardized test scores for consideration. You will also find colleges where admission review is *test blind*, that is, they never review test scores for admission, or *test flexible*, that is, they allow an array of tests to satisfy the requirement.

1. Visit FairTest, the National Center for Fair and Open Testing (https://www.fairtest.org), and find the Optional List of colleges and universities that do not require testing for admission review. How many schools are on this list? _____

2. Find three colleges in your state, or choose three you have researched or visited that are on the list. Go to their admission web pages to find out how they consider testing in the review process.

3. Fill in the table below with the information requested in the bullet points.
   - The factors the school uses to make decisions other than standardized tests.
   - The percentage of applicants who chose to be reviewed without test scores (i.e., test-optional applicants).
   - The percentage of applicants admitted last year without testing.
   - *Note: If you do not see this level of detail on a college's site, you will need to call or email to get the answers. This is important information and worth your time. In fact, you should always reach out to schools when you have questions.*

College name	Factors considered	Percentage of applicants without test scores	Percentage of admitted applicants without test scores

4. Search online to find a college in your state that is test blind or test flexible, or look for one among schools you have visited or among those that have sent you promotional material via email or mail.

Note: Even if you ultimately decide to take both the SAT and ACT, it is important to know your options and understand how colleges differ in their policies and review. Remember that optional means optional, so you could decide to send your scores to some of the test-optional colleges you apply to and not to others.

Institution Investigation

It is time to look into how colleges make their admission decisions. In the next chapter, we will dive into holistic admission, but let's start with schools that use formulaic review to see how they review your grades and test scores and to see if they evaluate anything beyond the GPA on your school's official transcript.

Before we proceed, it is important to understand that the vast majority of colleges will combine your highest section scores across all the dates on which you took the SAT or the ACT, instead of looking only at your scores from any one time you took the test. This combining of the best section scores across multiple tests is known as *superscoring*. The example below illustrates the superscore from two test administrations of the ACT.

	Reading	Math	English	Science	Composite
June ACT	30	28	29	30	29
September ACT	28	30	30	29	29
Superscored ACT	30	30	30	30	30

Use this table to list your current SAT or ACT scores (the top row is an example).

SAT/ACT	Date	Subscores	Total score
SAT	9/2021	680 Math / 660 EBRW	1340

Note: EBRW stands for *evidence-based reading and writing*, which is the SAT's term for the merged scores from the Reading and Writing sections.

If you have taken either test more than once, what is your superscore after combining the highest subscores?

SAT _____

ACT _____

Index Exercise

Go online and search for either "Regents Admission Index and Iowa" or "Admission requirements and the California State System" or "Georgia and Freshman Index." What information are you able to find related to graduation requirements? In other words, which courses must you have taken in high school to be eligible for admission to these schools? List those below.

What can you learn about these state university systems' ACT and SAT requirements for admission? And do these vary based on your GPA?

Are you able to determine if admission requirements ever vary based on your major?

In general, what takeaways do you have about how formulaic admission review processes work in these, and presumably other, state university systems?

What other questions does this exercise bring up for you about the overall college admission review process? Include those and other notes below.

Closer to home

Does your state university system have a published and public admission formula? If so, do all schools in the system use it or only a subset?

Find a college or university within a few hours' driving distance of your home that uses a formulaic admission review. Are you admissible according to its stated criteria?

Final Thoughts

After this investigation, we are confident you will be able to find at least one college to add to your list that offers a major you find interesting, that is located in an area that appeals to you, and that would admit you with your current grades and test scores through its formulaic review.

6.7

Family Forward

I (Rick) do not remember all of the conversations I had with family, friends, and colleagues when my wife was pregnant, but the majority of them were congratulatory and encouraging. However, before each of our kids was born, I vividly remember getting a few comments that were sobering. These were not the common jests of "Sleep now because that's over" or "Good luck. Call me when they are seven or eight, and I will come babysit."

No. These were the sort that stung. Here are two that people actually wrote in baby shower cards: "Even if you do sleep when they are born, you will never really rest again" and "Parenting is simultaneously heaven and hell. Your job is to . . ." And below that, they had just signed their initials.

My point is that raising kids is a balancing act that makes us continually question our judgment, role, and, at times, very sanity. How much do you do for them? When do you let them take over or fall or fail so that they can learn and grow? What are the *right* words? Is this the right time to say them? Or is it better to revisit the situation later? Perhaps all of that is what the message meant in pointing out the difference between *sleep* and *rest*. We worry about them. We question ourselves. And ultimately we come to realize there is no blueprint for parenting. And perhaps the other message had more wisdom than warning in saying "Your job is to . . . " In many ways the job of parenting regularly requires balancing two worlds, navigating with incomplete information, and basically never stopping.

In this chapter, we have asked your student to do a good bit of research. We asked them to review their high school's profile, their current transcript, and their high school course choices, and we also asked them to look into how colleges make formulaic admission decisions.

We are not going to walk you through all of that. Instead, in this Come Together, we are going to ask you to walk that fine line of parenting: to trust them and stretch them, simultaneously. We want you to play the role of learner. We want you to be curious about all they have been digging into without being pushy in your questions. Easy? No. Extremely important? Yes. You got this!

Here are a few of the topics you can ask your student about:

- Grade trends

- Rigor of curriculum

- Primary differences between the ACT and SAT

- Superscoring

- Test-optional and test-blind admission

- Primary difference between formulaic admission and holistic admission

- What have they learned about the admission review of colleges they are interested in?

- How has what they have learned informed their search or application experience?

- What do they need (and not need) from you?

If you have not heard this lately, we say thank you. Thanks for loving your kids and supporting them. Thanks for walking with them when you do not have all the answers and are constantly trying to balance and reconcile roles and responsibilities. Remember the ellipsis in your job description (Your job is to . . .). Embrace the uncertainty that comes with parenting, and enjoy the opportunity to figure this out together.

6.8

Come Together

Students, it is your show today. We have prepped your family with some questions to ask, but we are counting on you to take a good fifteen to thirty minutes to walk them through the lessons you learned in this chapter. Look back over your notes and research about high school profiles, transcripts, rigor of curriculum, grade trends, and the factors weighed in formulaic admission review. Review your takeaways from the podcast episodes on the ACT and SAT. How might all the details you dug into influence your next steps?

Parents, after you hear more about your student's lessons learned in this chapter, is there anything we covered in Family Forward (6.7) that you would like to ask about?

We hope you will set aside time as a family to discuss these questions:

How has your approach to the application experience shifted since
  beginning the workbook?

What else do you want to learn more about?

Test Planning and Preparation

Now that you have more information about how colleges review your academic record, and you understand the basic differences between the two main standardized tests, you should evaluate your testing plan going forward.

1. If you have not already taken one of the tests, what do you need to do to register?

2. If you have taken one of the tests, are you planning to take the other or retake the same one?

3. Look up the schedule to learn when and where the exams will be administered in your area. Decide who will register and when, and be sure you record these dates on your calendar.

4. Are you considering formal test preparation? If so, what do you need to discuss or arrange in order to schedule and pay for that service?

Fill in the table on the next page, or create your own, with the colleges and universities you are considering. Be sure at least one school uses formulaic admission review. In addition to recording all the schools' published test ranges and GPA averages, consider their admit rate and your academic profile. In chapter 7, we will discuss nonacademic factors used in holistic admission review, but based purely on your academic credentials, classify each college as a *reach* (you fall below the average admitted student profile), a *target* (you fall squarely in the average profile), or a *likely* (you exceed the formulaic review benchmarks). Discuss your classification as a family and with your school counselor to see whether they agree.

College name	GPA range and average	Test score range and average	Test optional (Y/N)	First-year class size	Admit rate	Likely, target, or reach

Chapter 7

Admission Factors II

WHAT ARE COLLEGES LOOKING FOR OUTSIDE THE CLASSROOM?

If chapter 6 felt a little dry and overly quantitative to you, welcome to something entirely different. If you love spreadsheets, formulas, and following recipes or manuals to a predictable conclusion, this may not be your favorite chapter because we are about to delve deeply into a gray area.

What are schools that use holistic admission looking for? A little bit of everything. Why? Because they can. Just kidding . . . sort of. Actually, it is because they receive far more applications from academically talented students than they have space available in their class. In other words, selective college admission, like the foundation of our economy, comes down to supply and demand.

Schools receiving thousands of applications for hundreds of seats in their first-year class add components to their review process in order to enroll students who will not only thrive academically but will also build a campus community that advances the institutional mission and enriches the experiences of others on campus. To do this, the schools require information from applicants geared toward revealing who they are outside the classroom. The schools want to know how you spend your time, details about your goals and motivations, examples of your character, and ways you have improved the lives of others around you. Essentially, they want to hear more from, and about, you.

Let's jump into helping you understand what to expect if you are applying to colleges that review your background *beyond the numbers.*

7.1

The Four *I*'s

Here are the fundamental questions that admission officers are asking when they review your Activities section of the application:

Question 1: What is this student *involved* in outside the classroom?

On your application, you will be asked not only to list *what* you participated in while in high school but also to quantify the *amount* of time per week or year that you invested in each activity. This includes clubs, organizations, work, volunteering, and other experiences. In the grid below, list some of the ways you have been involved in your school, family, or community during high school.

Activity	Years involved	Weeks/year	Hours/week
Ex: Druid Town High School Basketball	9, 10, 11, 12	14	20

Notice that we asked you to consider how you have been involved in your family during high school. Many students underestimate the value that colleges place on these less quantifiable activities. Not all students have a family activity to list, but, for instance, if you have been caring for younger siblings, working and contributing to your family's income, or translating for your parents in their personal or professional life, we encourage you to list that contribution and decide later if it is something you want to include in Activities, write about in an application essay, or discuss in an interview.

Tip 1. Admission officers are reading quickly. List the activity you care about the most first.

Tip 2. Be specific in the activity's name. Do not, for example, simply write "Basketball."

Tip 3. Do not use acronyms that are not well known. Do not, for example, write "CAN" for Community Action Network.

Question 2: What did this student *invest* in during high school?

For each activity you listed above, we want you to think about *how* you have contributed. Have you founded a club, held an elected position in one, been promoted at work, started a new tradition at school, or helped your family in a significant way? On your application you will have an opportunity to describe your investment. Use the grid below to expound on your involvement. *Note*: You should include personal and collective achievements where appropriate.

Activity	Achievements, position, and year
Ex: Druid Town High School Basketball	MVP in 10 District champions in 11 Captain in 12

Tip 1. Think beyond traditional positions. If you contributed in some unique way to a project or goal, mention that.

Tip 2. If you or a group accomplished something that you are proud of, list that.

Tip 3. Make note if the activity involved you being nominated or selected to participate.

Question 3: What *impact* has this student made?

Lots of students have "done stuff" in high school. If you are applying to more selective schools, admission readers will not only expect to see your involvement and investment but also to understand how your presence made something better. Again, they are trying to imagine you on their campus. Busy is not their barometer. They will admit students who are improving their community and the lives of those around them. In order to flesh this out, use your top activity from the grid above to answer five questions.

Activity:	
What problem did I face/solve?	
What lesson did I learn?	
What skill did I gain?	
How did I grow/improve?	
How did I improve the organization/others?	

Tip 1. Impact is an action, so use words that show this. Rather than write, "student council member," be specific: "advocated on behalf of the student body for . . ."

Tip 2. Don't overdo it. "Changed lives through volunteering" is a little much. Find a midway between understating and being grandiose.

Question 4: How has this student *influenced* others?

OK. Let's put all of this together now. Remember: your goal is to use strong, specific words (particularly verbs) and to be concise. Because you will have only 150 characters, do not write in full sentences. Take a crack at this in the box below for at least one of your activities.

Activity	Description (150 characters max)

Tip 1: Be aware of any redundancy. If you have already listed a position or achievement, do not simply restate it.

Tip 2: You don't need to describe the details of common activities; rather, explain the specific role you had.

Final Tips

Write down the schedule for your average week. Are there ways you fill your time that you are overlooking?

Revisit, rethink, rework, revise. If we had to boil it down to one question that admission readers are asking when they review your Activities section, it is this: **Will this student be missed when they graduate?**

Just like with your essays (which we will talk about next), you can always revise and improve your activity descriptions. Think of the Activities section like you would any longer form of writing. At the same time, be succinct in your explanations and avoid fluff. After you write your descriptions initially, walk away from them and come back a day later to read and consider them again:

Did I leave out any accomplishments, awards, or opportunities? Are there other lessons learned that I neglected to include?

Is my language specific? Are there any redundancies?

Are there any acronyms someone outside my school or community would not be familiar with?

Can I use my limited space more strategically?

Did I acquire any skills I could include to demonstrate growth?

Gather input. Show these grids to your parents, a friend, sibling, and teacher or counselor who knows you well. Are your descriptions clear? Are you missing anything? Sometimes students fail to list activities or responsibilities because doing them is just part of their routine and they don't think to mention them. Colleges want to know these pieces.

Essay Ease

In presentations and individual meetings, we regularly ask students which part of the application makes them the most nervous. Often and understandably, they cite the essay because it can feel like the last piece of the application they fully control. This is likely why books have been written about the application essay, and consultants make a living from helping students "craft," "perfect," or "tailor" their writing. We are here to give you practical tips and advice. You will need to "do the work," but we will walk you through how to do it well.

Getting Started

Often we hear students say that just getting started is the most challenging part of writing the essay. Our friend and colleague Brian K. Smith is the dean of college counseling and an English instructor at Marlborough School in Los Angeles, California. Having taught and counseled students at schools around the country, he says, "I try to teach my students *not to focus on what you think* the reader wants to hear, but, instead, focus more on *what speaks to you.*" He asks students, "*What is your truth and your story to tell?*" Ultimately, that is the definition of authenticity. Your story, your truth. If you listen to admission officers talk, they are constantly saying, "We just want to hear your authentic voice."

Free writing—the practice of simply getting words on paper—is the technique Mr. Smith uses to help his students get there.

How it works. Start by writing absolutely anything down on paper. Take whatever comes to mind and write about it. Your thoughts may be complex or simple, focused or flitting. Sit down and get on paper (or the screen) how you are feeling at the moment. Sometimes prompts help. Try this series of words, or randomly pick your own, and write for ten minutes without stopping: *running, exercise, food, calories, diet.*

The point is to keep going and not to stop writing. It doesn't matter if you stay on topic. This technique allows your mind to explore freely and can help tap into your creative juices. Mr. Smith likens free writing to his other passion, music. He says free writing is very much like warming up to sing a solo or in a choir. One of the first things a vocal coach will ask you to do is practice your scales to warm up your voice. Free writing works the same way, except instead of warming up your voice, you are tuning your brain to generate ideas on a topic.

Round two of free writing: take ten minutes and write what comes to your mind when you read one or two of these phrases:

Dinner at our house . . . Sunday mornings . . .

My proudest moment was . . . A victory I had was . . .

My most embarrassing moment was . . . The most difficult time of my life was . . .

The person I admire most is . . . What I recall vividly about my sibling is . . .

An adventure I had was . . . My best birthday was . . .

My number one dream for the future is . . . If I could do anything right now, I would . . .

The person who taught me the most is . . . If I could be with anyone right now, it would be . . .

If you do this exercise regularly in preparation for writing the essay, ideas flow and can turn into topics. Those topics turn into paragraphs, and those paragraphs can turn into well-constructed pieces of prose.

7.3

Topic Test

Now that you are ready to write, what should you write about? Admission officers love to use the word *passion*. We can't tell you how many times we have heard this somewhat trite tip: "Just write about your passion." Most of the time we are not even sure *they* know what that means. The other thing admission officers commonly say is "We just want to hear your voice." OK. So . . . passion and voice. How does that help you in selecting a topic? Actually, it doesn't, and in some ways that is a good thing.

The college essay is not a test to see if you can read minds or anticipate what admission officers want to hear. The personalities of admission officers vary. What mood they will be in or whose essay they will have read immediately before yours is not something you can control. Bottom line: write the essay for you, not them. In plain and simple terms, they want to know about you, how well you write, and how self-aware you are. In contrast, essays that are a wasted opportunity simply reiterate what you included in the Activities section and read like a resume in paragraph form.

In some cases you may be able to choose your topic. Often, however, you will be provided with several prompts and asked to choose one or two. As you look over your options, our advice is to pick one that will help you communicate these things:

- what you care about

- how you think

- how you have grown and learned over time

Reverse-engineer the essay. Don't read the essay questions; read yourself. Remember that your goal is to write something you believe in and are genuinely interested in.

Ask yourself these questions before you even look at the prompts:

What brings me joy?

What gets me excited or fired up?

If I had ninety seconds to convince someone to see things my way, what would I talk about?

What or who has changed my life?

When have I been most afraid, happy, fulfilled, or proud?

Now look at the prompts to see if one aligns with something you have already identified in your mind.

Committee Considerations

If more than one prompt seems interesting to you, being aware of the admission committee's mindset may help you decide which is the better choice. Here is what the admission committee is likely asking themselves when reading your essay:

Does this essay provide new insight or understanding into the student's life, motivations, values, character, or intentions?

Is there evidence of growth, maturity, or self-awareness?

Is this essay compelling, unique, and reflective?

Would this voice add value on our campus?

Final Filter

✓ Confirm that what you write reveals more about you than the other people or places in the story. Make sure your focus is on you and your life to this point, rather than on what you think life will or could be in college. Let the reader figure out fit or match, instead of trying to lead them down a path.

✓ Do not feel compelled to conclude with a lesson learned or a happy ending. You are sharing your story, not a fairy tale.

✓ Perfection—in college admission and in life—is often overvalued. Perfection should not be the goal in writing your essay. What will distinguish your writing and your application is your unique voice. Be willing to take risks, be vulnerable, and share your truth. Readers will appreciate the opportunity to learn more about you, and you will get to know yourself better as well.

Advice from Todd Rinehart, vice chancellor for enrollment at the University of Denver: *Students should know that while essays are important, they are rarely the reason a student gets admitted or denied. Students shouldn't feel the pressure of having to write a Pulitzer-winning essay to gain admission to their college of choice. With that said, they also need to know that an award-winning piece won't supersede poor academic performance. Most admission committees are looking for capable and competitive students academically—once academic ability is vetted, an essay plays an important role in helping committees build their class with interesting classmates and roommates. Committees aren't looking for the perfect essay, topic, or set of activities and achievements—we simply want an interesting, authentic, and well-written glimpse into a student's life.*

7.4

Short Answers

Many colleges will ask you to respond to short-answer questions with "supplemental essays" in addition to the main essay. In some cases you will have a choice of several prompts, while in others you will not. While all of the tips and strategies from sections 7.2 and 7.3 apply, you will need to be even more succinct because the word limit is typically far lower (often 150–300 words).

Here are examples of prompts:

"Tell a story from your life, describing an experience that either demonstrates your character or helped to shape it." *University of Washington*

"What is the hardest part of being a teenager now? What's the best part? What advice would you give a younger sibling or friend (assuming they would listen to you)?" *Rutgers University*

"Please share an experience that made you feel uncomfortable or challenged, and then explain how you grew from the situation." *Gonzaga University*

"The Hawaiian word *moʻolelo* is often translated as "story," but it can also refer to history, legend, genealogy, and tradition. Use one of these translations to introduce yourself." *Dartmouth College*

Choose one of the prompts above or search online for a supplemental essay question from a college that interests you. Before you start drafting a response, jot down some answers to the following questions:

1. How can I respond to this question honestly and specifically?

2. In what way does my understanding of this college impact how I approach this question? How can I show I am a good match?

3. Is there a way to refer or at least allude to how my background, experience, contributions, or perspective will benefit the campus community?

4. How can my response reflect my growth as a person or a student?

5. What might an admission reader be looking for beyond a straightforward answer to this question?

7.5

Why Us?

We began the workbook by asking you to consider *why* you are going to college. Now is the next phase of that thought process. Colleges are increasingly asking applicants to answer the question "Why us?" They know you are applying to multiple schools and want to know more about *how* your search process led you to them. They are trying to determine whether you are a good match for their community. Think about this like going to prom. There are a lot of people you could ask, but generally you ask someone you know, like, and have a sense may feel the same way (no additional charge or guarantees for our love advice). So while colleges will not call it the Prom Essay, it's the Prom Essay.

Here are two examples:

Why do you wish to attend Colorado College, and how would you contribute to the community? (no more than 200 words)

The University [of Minnesota] values diversity, broadly defined to include diversity of experiences, perspectives, backgrounds, and talents. Enrolling a diverse community of scholars interested in learning with and from each other fosters discussion and discovery inside and outside of the classroom. Please share briefly how you might contribute to, or benefit from, our community of scholars. (150 words)

Give it a shot.

Think about just one of the colleges you are interested in. Why is it on your list? Do not skip this. Think back to Mr. Smith's free writing exercise in 7.2, and take five minutes to get your free-association words and honest thoughts out.

Prom On

Our friend and colleague Dr. Michael Trivette, cofounder of College Transitions and coauthor of *Colleges Worth Your Money*, puts it this way: "It's your job as the writer to demonstrate how your interests align with the college's offerings and why you would be a perfect addition to their campus community." He offers students these tips:

1. **Show you did your homework.** If you find that you can simply replace the name of the college in the essay and have it work for every college you're applying to, you're doing it wrong. Instead, focus on specific things about the college that resonate with you. Perhaps it is the opportunity to work with Professor Moore on a nonverbal communication research project. Being drawn to the field of communication, you also cite the opportunity to study abroad in Poland while earning credit toward an intercultural communication course (COM 2124), and you mention the benefits provided through this experience. By finding a way to tie in this specific professor, a research project, a specific course, and a study abroad opportunity, you've now demonstrated to the reader that you've done your homework.

2. **Keep it personal.** Remember that admissions officers often read through hundreds, if not thousands, of college applications. If your essay is filled with statements about you wanting to attend this college because you think it's "great" and "has a stellar reputation," application readers may have to reach for another cup of coffee just to stay awake. When they say they are looking to "hear your voice" they mean that they want you to be clear and specific about why you want to go to their college. If anyone could have written the same 150 words, you have not done your job. Don't be the twenty-sixth applicant that day to mention the school's ranking in *U.S. News and World Report*, or they may stop reading and reach for a double shot of espresso instead.

3. **Ditch the nonessential details.** Many essays contain the equivalent of "I can visualize myself walking through Tech's arboretum after a long day of classes." Generally speaking, you want to provide better reasons for why you want to attend a school than its beauty, landmarks, or attractions. While there's nothing inherently wrong or off-putting about mentioning the weather, sports, campus buildings, or other campus or local attractions, it can eat up precious words to the short-response prompts.

How do these tips change what you wrote originally?

━━━━━━━━━━━━━ **7.6** ━━━━━━━━━━━━━

Writing Right

As we said earlier, students commonly say the essay and other writing is what makes them the most anxious about their application. While we hope the insight and exercises we have provided in this chapter have helped you think about what makes a compelling essay or short-answer response, we also know you may still feel a little uneasy. As you are working on your applications, and certainly before you hit submit, follow these recommendations.

1. **Answer the question**. Does this sound as ridiculous to read as it did to write? Every year, EVERY year, there are students who submit essays and short-answer questions that are completely unrelated to the prompt. When your friend's mom asks what you want for dinner, would you say, "seventeen"? Then why would anyone write an off-topic college essay? C'mon! This is the most basic of basics. At many colleges and scholarship programs, this is the first line in the rubric for scoring your essay: "Does the student answer the question?" Don't start in a hole. Just because you wrote a paper three weeks ago of the same length for your history class and got an A does not mean you should press CTRL+C and paste that thing into your college application. So pause, reread the prompt, and make sure you truly *answer the question*.

2. **Get to the point**. Your first sentence matters. Admission readers *always* start on your side. They are naturally curious. They begin reading every essay hoping it is good. Your job is to keep them with you. The first sentence of every paragraph matters. Many readers skim. Don't you? If you had been reading thirty to fifty essays a day for weeks on end, you would want some punch in the first line too, right? You would want the first paragraph to have detail and be specific and lead you into the rest of the essay, right? See, these people are not so different from you. Don't bury the lead or waste a bunch of time and words when you have so few for most of these prompts. *Get to the point.*

3. **Print it out**. Let's be honest. We've all sent a text or an email with a misspelled word or two put words in the wrong order. (See what we did there?) Sometimes you look at a computer screen for so long that your writing sounds good in your head but could be clearer or better stated. After your first draft, and again before you submit your application, print out your essays and short answers to questions. By changing your

perspective, you will see ways to improve, catch mistakes, and feel more confident as a result. Trust us: *print it out*.

4. **Read it out loud**. Once you print your essay out, grab your phone. Go to the voice notes app and hit record. Now read your essay and listen to it once or twice. We are guessing you don't even make it through the first eighty-five words without pausing to revise. That's a good thing. Keep reading and listening to it until you are satisfied. This is your best simulation of how an admission reader will hear your voice in your writing. Does doing this feel a little awkward and uncomfortable? Sorry. Sometimes awkward and uncomfortable are two steps on the path toward improvement. *Read it out loud*.

5. **Drop it on the floor**. Be sure your name is not on your essay, and drop it on the floor in one of your classes. If a friend or classmate picks it up and cannot return it to you after scanning it, you have not been detailed or specific enough. After all, if someone who knows you in a class of twenty cannot figure out it is yours, how will it fare in an applicant pool of twenty thousand? (While this suggestion is more figurative, we welcome you to try it literally.)

6. **Pass it on**. Did your essay hit its mark? Have you effectively communicated who you are and what you value? The best way to tell is to have your parents or a friend give a draft of your essay to a colleague or individual who has never met you. Ask the person to read the essay and respond with three adjectives that describe you and with a sentence that captures what they learned. Does the response reflect the message you hope to convey? If not, it is time to rethink it.

7. **Get it done**. Ask colleges what percentage of last year's applicants applied on the day of or the day before the deadline. You will frequently hear answers of well over 50 percent (often with hundreds coming in during the final few hours). We are pretty sure the last-minute submissions are due to students obsessing over their essay. An essay is not an unhatched egg. Sitting on it does not help. You know what does? *Following numbers 1–6 above*.

You cannot control exactly who reads your essay. You cannot be assured yours will be the best one in the applicant pool or the thing that gets you in, but if you follow these tips, we are confident you will have written an excellent essay or short-answer response. So after you have taken your writing through these steps, breathe deeply and move on.

7.7

Additional Information

While other sections of the college application provide examples or detailed instructions, the "Additional Information" or "Special Circumstances" portion is intentionally open-ended. It is included and designed to provide space for applicants to explain experiences they may have had in their life that they could not write about elsewhere in the application. This can give admission readers important contextual information that helps them understand an applicant's life and background better.

That may sound straightforward, but students often have questions about how or whether to complete this section and how colleges incorporate it into their review of your application. These are questions we often hear: *Can I include one of the essays here that I could not fit anywhere else? Will leaving this blank hurt me? Is this another way to demonstrate interest?*

First, this is not a required section. Second, it is not intended to trip you up. It simply gives you a little extra space to communicate necessary *whys* or *what elses*—critical pieces of information that can provide valuable context (inside or outside the classroom) you were not able to convey elsewhere. Therefore, understandably, most students do not find it necessary to complete the section. In short, leaving it blank is not only fine; it is common.

Here is how you can figure out if there is anything critical in your background to describe in this section. Jot down quick responses or make a few bullet points under any that apply to you:

1. Have there been critical events in your life or family that the application has not allowed you to describe? (Think about personal circumstances that have disrupted your high school experience in a significant way. These may include a health issue, death in your immediate family, or natural disaster.)

2. Were your academic choices or opportunities impacted during high school because of changing schools, unavoidable schedule conflicts, or course cancellations?

3. Did the Activities section limit your ability to fully articulate your notable achievements or the extent to which you contributed? (Remember that this is "additional" for you and, to an extent, is additional for admission committees too. Hint: Put your strongest, most compelling information *first* in Activities. Do not run over into Additional Information unless it is absolutely essential to convey the depth of your work or time. Don't be redundant.)

4. Are there inconsistencies in your academic performance that need further explanation?

Before you complete your application, read it over in its entirety. Ask yourself these questions:

Is there something else, something missing, or something imperative an admission committee needs to know that I have not discussed?

Is the Additional Information section an appropriate place to include that information, or am I able to work it in elsewhere in the application?

7.8

Interview Intel

Whether you have a required or an optional interview with an admission officer, a faculty member, an alum, or a current student, here is what you need to know.

What the interviewer wants:

- to know more about you than what is on paper
- for you to be prepared
- to learn details and specifics about you
- to discuss your motivations and goals

What the interviewer doesn't want:

- to ask all the questions
- for you to be overly scripted
- for you to list accomplishments as though you are reading off your resume

Ultimately, your goal is to demonstrate through your responses, body language, and the questions you pose about the college that you are genuinely interested in it and would be a great addition to the campus community. And here is the good news and the most important truth to keep in mind as you prepare for interviews: interviewers want you to do well. They love their school and are excited to talk to students who are interested in it.

We understand you may still get nervous on the day of your interview, but if you prepare by using the activities in this section, and keep in mind that the person asking you questions is internally rooting for you, you are going to do a great job. Let's get started.

Resume Review

If you do not already have a resume, we suggest you create one. You will find a number of great templates to choose from online. We suggest you continue to update your resume throughout high school. Not only will having one help tremendously when you complete the Activities section of your application, but you will also find that college admission and scholarship interviewers will often ask you to send one in advance of your interview as well. Give your resume to a family member, classmate, or friend and ask them to skim it.

a. What is the first thing their eyes go to?

b. What information do they think is missing, unclear, or misleading?

c. Did they find any misspellings, punctuation missing or incorrectly used, or formatting (including fonts and the use of bolding/italics/underlining) that is distracting?

d. Have them ask you two questions based on information they found on your resume. Provide responses thirty to forty-five seconds long.

Based on feedback you receive . . .

Are there edits you can make to improve your resume?

Is there a different option you believe will help tell your story more effectively? (Take some time to search online to view other templates and layouts.)

Practice Makes . . . Better

OK. Now that you are warmed up, let's start to refine your answers and get you feeling more comfortable in your responses. Get out your phone and voice-record a response to a few of these prompts.

- What is the most significant contribution you have made to a club, team, your family, community, or school?

- What would your teachers say are your greatest strengths as a person and as a student?

- What is one thing you would change about your high school?

- What do you like about your high school?

- What might you study in college?

- What has been your favorite subject in high school? Why?

- Tell me about a book you have read or a movie you have seen recently.

- What are some of your personal and career goals for the future?

- What do you enjoy doing in your free time?

- How would you describe yourself as a person?
- What events would you say have been crucial to your life thus far? What people?
- Tell me about one of your heroes.
- Why are you interested in our college?
- What do you think you will contribute to a college campus?
- Have you ever thought of not going to college right away? What would you do?
- If you could talk to any one person past or present, to whom would you talk? Why?

Label each response separately and save them on your phone. Wait at least one day before going back and listening to each, and make quick notes to these questions as you do:

What do you wish you had included?

Is there anything you think you could have said differently or omitted?

Few people like the sound of their own voice, but pay attention to your volume, tone, pace, and word choice.

What stands out as positive and compelling?

What stands out as unclear or unconfident?

Good news! You get to do it again. Choose at least one or two of your responses, and record a new answer. After you have done this, ask the same questions you walked through after initially listening to your responses.

Do you hear improvement?

What lessons can you apply to any question you are asked from this exercise?

There is no perfect length of time for answering questions. However, you want to find a balance between being specific and thorough and yet not rambling or using a lot of time for any one question.

Check the time you spent answering each question.

If you had to add fifteen seconds or cut fifteen seconds from each, how would you do it?

After listening to your shortest and longest responses, do you get a sense of the "sweet spot" for time in those answers?

Practice Makes . . . Better-er

Likely based on Dr. Albert Mehrabian's research on nonverbal communication in the 1950s, Will Smith's character in the movie *Hitch* says, "60 percent of all human communication is nonverbal, 30 percent is your tone, so that means that 90 percent of what you're saying ain't coming out of your mouth." Regardless of the precise percentages, there is no doubt that your message is more than your words. We know that you experience this every day in the body language you see friends, teachers, family members, politicians, or celebrities exhibit.

If you did not enjoy listening to your voice responses, you may like this next suggestion even less. Remember that you are your own biggest critic, so stay objective, relax, and apply what you have learned here.

Pick between three and five of the prompts you are most excited to discuss and either use your phone to video-record yourself or ask a friend or family member to ask these questions and record you providing thirty- to forty-five-second responses to each. Again, wait at least one day before watching your recording. Then make quick notes to these questions:

What do you notice about your posture?

Do your hand gestures enhance or distract from your answers?

Are you looking directly into the camera, or does your eye contact stray?

What makes you the most pleased with or proud of your video?

What do you want to change or improve?

Check the time you spent answering each question.

If you had to add fifteen seconds or cut fifteen seconds from each, how would you do it?

After watching your shortest and longest response, do you get a sense of the "sweet spot" for time in those answers?

Rinse and repeat: rerecord at least one or two of your videos.

Do you see improvement?

What lessons can you apply to any question you are asked from this exercise?

Extra credit: If you did not have someone ask you the questions initially, send your clips to a counselor, friend, family member, or someone else whose opinion you value. Ask them to answer the same questions you did after watching your responses.

The Wrap-up

We hope you are feeling more and more comfortable talking about yourself at this point. It is not easy. Ultimately, your job is to promote yourself without coming across as arrogant. Answer the questions, but do not ramble. Be prepared, but do not sound scripted. We know. We know. That is a lot to ask. You are just going to have to trust us—and more importantly—trust yourself. You are ready.

While you can never predict every topic an interviewer will ask you about, there is one question sure to come after they have gone through their battery of questions. And spoiler alert, it will be in every interview you ever have: *What questions do you have for me?*

That one is sneaky important because while it is genuine and straightforward, it also comes with an agenda. The question tests your ability to demonstrate preparedness, curiosity, and genuine interest. *Do not* start with basic questions you could find the answers to with a visit to the university's home page: "What is your mascot?" or "How many students are on campus?"

Instead, illustrate that you have done your homework by asking about topics such as these:

- The research of a certain professor.
- More details about the major you are considering.
- The student culture or community culture.
- Reference an article you read in the college's student newspaper or alumni magazine.
- Ask the interviewer what they would change about the school.

Take some time to dig into the materials a college has sent you or to explore its website. Come up with three questions that you genuinely want to answers to. Not only is this good preparation for your interview; but also, if you cannot formulate three questions, it may be a clue that the school is not a good match.

7.9

Letters of Recommendation

We understand that you will not be writing your own letters of recommendation (LORs). If this is something you had considered doing . . . don't. Still, it is important that you understand why LORs are components of holistic review and how you can help your teachers and counselors submit effective letters on your behalf.

In your application, you have provided critical information to an admission committee about your background, involvement, and academic performance; and through your writing, you have touched on goals and motivations. Letters from counselors and teachers support and complement all of this. And they serve as an opportunity for adults in your current community to speak directly with adults in your future community about the character, skills, talents, and potential you will bring to college.

Selecting Recommenders

Most applications will require that you include a recommendation from your school counselor. Typically, though, you have more freedom to select the teachers who will write a recommendation for you.

Here are questions to ask as you decide whom to approach for a letter on your behalf.

Who can speak to my character, tenacity, diligence, grit, resilience, success, and failure?

Who is able to describe my growth and contributions inside and/or outside the classroom?

Who may be able to fill in holes, add context and color, or articulate my impact in a unique, compelling voice?

After considering these questions, list at least two or three possible recommenders from different subject areas and grades. Ideally, the recommenders should know you from your junior or senior year.

Teacher name	Subject area	Grade level	Reason to ask

Regardless of whose name you included, here are two things you need to know about all teachers and counselors: (1) they want to help you, and (2) they have limited time. They are being asked to write LORs for lots of other students, in addition to their normal responsibilities.

Research Recommendation Requirements

Find the information on LORs for one of the colleges you are considering. Fill in the details in this grid or create your own.

College	
Website with information about LORs	
Deadline for application	
Deadline for LORs, if different	
Number of LORs required	
Subject / grade level specified or not	

You will find that while sometimes you have liberty in choosing your recommenders, often colleges want to hear from persons in certain roles. Go online and find details about LORs from one of the other colleges you are considering.

Are there differences in the number of recommendations required?

Do different teachers or community members seem better suited for one college versus another? Why?

Your school may have a system, template, and timeline for requesting recommendations. If that is not the case, use the Recommendation Request (7.10) or create and save a similar one. *Note*: We suggest setting your LOR request date at *least* a month in advance of the deadline so that you can give your recommenders adequate time to think about what they want to write and ask you any questions they might have. Use this table or create your own to track deadlines, with your LOR request date set a month ahead of when the applications and recommendations are due.

College name / website	Application deadline	LOR request date	Recommender name

Requesting Your Recommendations

Remember what we discussed earlier. These folks want to help you. But they are also spread extremely thin. Well in advance of application deadlines, ask them in person if they would be willing to write a letter of recommendation on your behalf. Then schedule a meeting with your teacher. Prior to your discussion, email them your resume; you should also bring a hard copy of the resume with you on the day of your appointment.

Your goal is to have a productive and honest conversation with your teachers. Write down answers to these questions in advance, and either show this to them or cover this information in your meeting:

Why I am asking you

Why I am applying to this college

Why I am interested in this major

What I am proudest of that I hope you have seen

What I hope you will be able to touch on

When you do sit down with each recommender, start by thanking them. Acknowledge that their time is valuable and confirm that they are able to and comfortable with recommending you. This gives them the opportunity to express any concerns and ask you questions at the outset.

Ultimately you cannot control exactly how your recommendations will read, but if you try these activities, we are confident you are doing everything you can to ensure this part of your application is strong.

Waiving Your Right

On the forms for requesting recommendations in the application, you will be asked to respond to a Family Educational Rights and Privacy Act waiver. You will have the choice to waive the right to see your application's recommendations. When prompted, we strongly encourage you to *waive your right*. Doing so demonstrates trust toward your recommenders. Also, some high schools have policies that prohibit recommenders from sending your materials if you have not waived your right of access.

Final note: The current counselor-to-student ratio in the United States is nearly 500:1 (double the ratio recommended by the National Association for College Admission Counseling). As with all other sections of your application, admission readers bear your context in mind. They know that, in large high schools, your time with a counselor or teachers is limited. If you are in a high school like that, be assured that committees will not hold a generic or brief LOR against you in their review.

7.10

Recommendation Request (Template)

Senior's name as it appears on applications _____

Date of birth _____

LETTER OF RECOMMENDATION INFORMATION FORM
*Seniors are to give a copy of this form to each teacher from whom they are
requesting a letter of recommendation. A request is to be made no less than
five weeks before any deadline.*

- -

Teacher's name _____

Date form is being given to teacher _____

School counselor _____ Faculty advisor _____

1. **List of people writing letters of recommendation**
   Teachers:

   Personal (outside school):

   Other:

2. **List of colleges and application deadlines**
   <u>Full name of college</u>   <u>Deadline</u>

3. **Topics or experiences the student hopes the teacher will include (optional):**
   What I remember about your class is . . .
   I am asking you to write this recommendation because . . .
   My proudest academic achievement is . . .

7.11

Family Forward

A few years ago, I (Rick) stopped coaching my son's 9-year-old-boys soccer team and moved on to my daughter's 7-year-old squad. Let's just say it was a . . . transition. The 9-year-olds, especially in those last few seasons, had really developed their skills and understanding of the game. We had progressed to using terms like *check*, *square*, and *drop*. When they came to practice, they would (generally) listen, execute the drills, and understand what I was instructing them to do.

It did not take me long to remember what coaching 7-year-olds was like. In the first practice, one girl literally fell to the ground when I yelled, "Drop!" (I'm not sure what she would have "checked" had I used that term). When I asked them to stand five yards apart and work on two-touch passing, I got a few blank stares combined with distances that left me wondering if it was their understanding of "five" or "yard" that we needed to work on.

And then we had our first game. It felt like trying to control foosball players verbally. I found myself calling out from the sideline, "Now you kick it to her, then you kick it to her, and . . ." Yeah. To say it did not work would be a massive understatement. On the ride home I realized I needed to rethink my approach and expectations.

In this chapter, we have walked your student through how to put their best foot forward in their applications to colleges that have holistic review. Your job as a parent is to coach, not play; to facilitate, not control; and to put them in a position to succeed. Here is how you can coach well through the application.

Evaluate Extracurricular Experiences and Activities

We suggested that your student create or update their resume to use when preparing for interviews, when completing the Activities portion of the application, and when asking teachers and counselors to write recommendation letters. In the spirit of a coach, we hope you will let them create and refine their own resume.

We do, however, encourage you to help keep track of the various activities your student has engaged in during high school, as well as any recognition, awards, or significant moments they may not remember or think to include when application season rolls around. While the exact format is up to you (an Excel spreadsheet or Word document works well), take fifteen minutes or so to create this record. We suggest beginning with the ninth grade and listing information for each grade separately.

After your student completes the Activities section of their application, offer to review it and ask yourself these questions:

Is the order of activities the most compelling? (The most interesting activities should come first.)

Are there opportunities to be more succinct or specific?

Is the information accurate?

Did they forget anything you believe is important?

Often students do not check capitalization, spelling, or formatting as diligently in this section as they do in their essays. Be sure to pay attention to those elements and offer corrections and suggestions.

Review Writing (Essays and Short-Answer Responses)

Having kids of our own, we completely understand the temptation to veer away from being an editor and move toward becoming a ghostwriter. Imagine a coach running onto the soccer field in the middle of a kids' game and blasting a shot past a hapless 7-year-old goalie. We know that image seems ridiculous. The truth is that in the essay and other writing portions of an application, admission officers are looking for what parents too often steal—the applicant's voice. Stay on the sideline, coach. Here is how.

Instead of editing your student's essay yourself, ask your student if they are comfortable with you sending it to one of your colleagues or friends who does not know your student well. Explain that this is a more accurate simulation of the admission review experience because this person is not emotionally connected to or familiar with the applicant.

Ask your invited reader to respond to these questions:

What was the most compelling point or line?

Was anything unanswered or unclear?

What are three adjectives you would use to describe the author?

Do you see an opportunity to be more specific?

If you had to cut anything, what would it be and why?

Did you find any misspellings or grammatical issues that need to be addressed?

While you may also want to review your student's essay, this is an opportunity for them to first consider feedback provided by an outside reader and make revisions. It also allows you to see how they respond and incorporate edits and feedback.

Additional Information and Special Circumstances

This section is designed for students to include details of their life they were unable to fit into other sections. While most applicants do not need or use this section, here is the one question you should ask in order to determine if it is applicable: *Has anything occurred during high school in the life of my student or our family that would help an admission committee gain important perspective or critical context?*

If the answer to this question is yes in your opinion, then you should have a conversation with your student about whether, where, and how they might include that in their application. This may or may not be the appropriate section. We trust that if you take the posture of a coach and not a player, making that determination will not be an issue.

Interviews

In this chapter we also provided your student with tips, strategies, and activities to help them prepare for interviews. It is natural for them to be nervous in advance. We have found one of the best ways to help students learn some of the key dos and don'ts of interviewing—and be able to relax prior to interviewing—is to tell them stories about the best and worst interviews you have been a part of in your life. Perhaps this was an interview you bombed. Perhaps you recall interviewing someone who was awkward, embarrassing, or otherwise memorable. Before your student interviews for admission or a scholarship, help them by sharing such stories with them.

Letters of Recommendation

When it comes to reviewing letters of recommendation, admission officers want to hear from teachers, counselors, or community members who can speak to a student's life in a rounded fashion:

- Character traits

- Patterns of behavior

- Growth, improvement, and resilience

- Role in a classroom, club, job, or team

- Approach to problems

- Self-awareness

- Involvement, impact, and influence inside and/or outside the classroom

- Ability to contribute to a college community

Admission officers *do not* care about recommenders having a big job title, and they do not want more recommendations than their application instructions asked for.

Being a coach is not easy, but it is a privilege. Our hope is that you continue to make *winning* less about the result of the game and more about building trust, staying connected, and supporting your student—holding them up and celebrating them, rather than trying to control them or achieve a particular outcome. In documentaries or press conferences, athletes do not talk about how their coach got them to something (a title, award, etc.) but how the coach got to them as a person—by building trust, believing in them, and encouraging them unfailingly. You have a good game plan now. Go get 'em, coach!

7.12

Family Investigation of Institutions

Find a college or university in your state or within a few hours driving distance of your home that utilizes a holistic admission review process. Read its description of application review.

1. What nonacademic criteria does the school give weight to?

2. What is its stated rationale for how the admission office reads and reviews applications?

Find a few colleges that use holistic review and offer the major your student is considering. Use the table below or create your own. The admit rates of the schools you include should vary. We also encourage you to find at least one university outside your state or geographic region. Put an X in the cell of any factors the schools use in their review of applications.

College name				
Admission website				
Admit rate				
Activities/ extracurriculars				
Essays				
Interview				
Letters of recommendation				
Other requirements/ factors				
Notes				

7.13
Come Together

Students: Look back over your notes from each section of this chapter. Here is what we would like you to do for your family members:

1. Explain why colleges consider multiple factors apart from GPA and test scores in holistic review: for example, extracurricular involvement, writing, and recommendations.

2. Discuss what they look for in each factor and how you think you can prepare to put your best foot forward with each section of an application.

3. Name one tip or insight you gained from your reading or research that surprised you.

4. What do you think will be your strongest and weakest nonacademic areas?

5. What makes you most excited and most nervous about applying based on the information in this chapter?

Coaches *(a.k.a. family members)*: After listening to your student's explanations and looking back over 7.11 and 7.12, discuss these questions:

1. What was your biggest takeaway from learning the components of holistic review?

2. How do you believe you can be most helpful in coaching your student through a holistic application review?

3. What makes you most excited and most nervous given what you learned in this chapter?

Walk your student through the research you did on various colleges in 7.12.

Discuss

a. What you learned

b. What surprised or confused you

c. Other schools you can research together

Chapter 8

Admission Decisions

In the 1984 classic film *The Karate Kid* (repopularized by the Netflix original *Cobra Kai*), Daniel LaRusso (Ralph Macchio) convinces Mr. Miyagi (Pat Morita) to train him in the martial art of karate. For the first several weeks, however, Daniel does not think he's learning anything because Mr. Miyagi has him doing only manual labor. He paints a fence, washes a car, and scrubs a deck for hours and hours. Finally, Mr. Miyagi shows Daniel how it all fits together—that "painting the fence" and "wax on, wax off" are actually defensive blocking techniques.

Are you ready to enter the admissions dojo? Good. Because in this chapter we are going to build on what you have already learned and connect the knowledge you have gained up to this point. First, let's recap what you already know.

You now have a bigger perspective on the higher education landscape. You know there are thousands of colleges and universities in our nation and abroad—the landscape is global, and your choices are vast. You know that most institutions are admitting more students than they deny and that many are strictly using academic criteria to make admission decisions: that is, they are operating in an outward-facing, transparent, and formulaic manner.

You know that the first principle of college admission is the same as that of microeconomics: supply and demand. The number of applications received for the number of spots available in a class is what drives the admit rate. If the quality and number of applicants go up, selectivity also goes up, and the admit rate goes down. Furthermore, you know that when the quality and number of applicants to a college increases, the college tends to add factors to its admission review and adopt a holistic process.

In the last two chapters, we covered what factors in your background colleges review and the conversations they are having in committee. In other words, you know what they are looking *at* and *for* in your application. In this chapter, we are going to delve into *how* are they actually making admission decisions.

The truth is that in a holistic process, *mission drives admission* decisions. Do not expect selective colleges simply to rate your essay, evaluate and score your activities, and then put those into a formula along with your grades and testing. Again, holistic means holistic. It means before they create, let alone review an application, they have specific goals or priorities that ultimately dictate their decisions. TRANSLATION: You will frequently find students admitted to selective schools who have lower numbers and weaker records of impact and influence in their community than a student who gets denied. Is this fair? No. But it is completely logical. That may sound as paradoxical as Mr. Miyagi's instruction sometimes seemed to Daniel. Let's keep training.

8.1
Mission Accepted

Admission deans and directors are not evaluated at the end of each year by how fair they have been but instead by the academic performance and retention rates of the classes they bring in, whether or not they have met enrollment targets, and if they have helped advance the mission and vision of the institution that their college president or board of trustees has established. Class goals start with a specified number of students in each class. If you are the dean or director of admission and your goal is two thousand first-year students, you know how many applicants to admit based on the percentage of students who typically accept your offer of admission (known as the *yield*).

EXAMPLE COLLEGE (Home of the Fighting Ex's):

Desired size of first-year class: 2,000; average yield: 37 percent; admit: ~5,425

Revenue models are built around total enrollment, so the overall number of students in a class is imperative. After that, however, all colleges have subgoals (the numbers within the macro-number) that you may hear referred to as "institutional priorities." These center around what that particular college wants to increase and improve. Logically, then, the institutional priorities of individual presidents or chancellors or boards will vary.

Example College's priorities

1. Grow the percentage of students from outside our region.

2. Diversify the number of countries from which we enroll students.

3. Double the number of students in our environmental science major.

If you are the dean of admission at Example College, those directives are going to influence your recruitment marketing and programs, as well as your admission process. While you will certainly never know the granularity of such goals, you can see the umbrella under which these are created by looking at mission statements.

Take a look at Caltech's mission statement, followed by Brown University's:

The mission of the California Institute of Technology is to expand human knowledge and benefit society through research integrated with education. We investigate the most challenging, fundamental problems in science and technology in a singularly collegial, interdisciplinary atmosphere, while educating outstanding students to become creative members of society.

The mission of Brown University is to serve the community, the nation and the world by discovering, communicating and preserving knowledge and understanding in a spirit of free inquiry, and by educating and preparing students to discharge the offices of life with usefulness and reputation. We do this through a partnership of students and teachers in a unified community known as a university-college.

1. What are the primary differences you notice between the mission statements of these two universities?

2. Based on their missions, do the schools seem to looking for any specific characteristics or priorities in the students they admit?

3. How would understanding a school's mission impact your approach to the application essay or short-answer prompts?

What can you infer about the admission policies of the University of Carolina, Chapel Hill, from its mission statement?

Our mission is to serve as a center for research, scholarship, and creativity and to teach a diverse community of undergraduate, graduate, and professional students to become the next generation of leaders. Through the efforts of our exceptional faculty and staff, and with generous support from North Carolina's citizens, we invest our knowledge and resources to enhance access to learning and to foster the success and prosperity of each rising generation. We also extend knowledge-based services and other resources of the University to the citizens of North Carolina and their institutions to enhance the quality of life for all people in the State.

With lux, libertas—light and liberty—as its founding principles, the University has charted a bold course of leading change to improve society and to help solve the world's greatest problems.

1. What does the mission statement tell you about what kind of student the school prioritizes in admission?

2. Research the admit rate and academic profile of in-state residents versus nonresidents. Can you see a correlation between mission and admission?

3. Would it surprise you to know that, in North Carolina, legislation exists mandating that no less than 82 percent of undergraduate students at schools in the public system must come from North Carolina?

Research two of the colleges you are interested in applying to or visiting.

1. What are some key words or phrases from their mission statements that stand out to you?

2. Write down some of your previous experiences or future goals that align with their missions.

3. How does knowing their missions prepare you for a possible interview or an essay or short-answer response?

4. What other questions does this review of mission statements bring up?

Now that you have seen a number of mission statements from colleges, it is time to develop your own. This is an expansion on your *why* from chapter 1.

Step 1. Start by writing words, phrases, or a sentence in response to these questions.

1. Why do you want to go to college?

2. What are you looking for in a particular college?

3. How do finances factor into your search and selection process?

4. What is ultimate success for you when you are looking back on your search and selection journey?

5. How do relationships with your family factor into your search and decisions for college?

Step 2. Review your answers and fill in the blanks below.

My mission in the college search, application, and selection journey is to

_____

_____.

Along the way I am committed to _____

_____.

Ultimately I want to attend a college that _____

_____.

As I finish high school and head to college, I hope my relationship with my family is characterized by

_____

_____.

Step 3. OK. Now take ten to fifteen minutes to incorporate your answers from both steps into two or three sentences.

Step 4. Sleep on it. Take a day or two and then revisit your mission statement.

What is missing?

What edits, changes, deletions, or improvements can you make that encapsulate what you (not anyone else) are truly hoping for in this experience?

Feel free to continue to tinker with your mission statement. We will be asking you to share this with your family later in this chapter.

8.2

Strategic Survey

While mission statements are tweaked occasionally, they are rarely radically changed. College presidents, however, will always create their own strategic plan when they arrive on campus. Because the average tenure of college presidents is under seven years ("The Slowly Diversifying Presidency" at https://www.insidehighered.com), you will find tremendous insight into their priorities and the culture they are attempting to build by reviewing those public documents online.

You do not need to read the entire plan. Check out the Executive Summary (typically the first few pages of a strategic plan) for one of the colleges you are considering.

1. What are your three biggest takeaways from reviewing the plan?

2. How might the plan impact the experience you would have at that school?

3. Are there specific characteristics, traits, or priorities you think admission readers may be looking for in students based on this plan?

4. Is there anything clearly stated about enrollment goals in the plan?

5. How would understanding a school's strategic plan impact your essay or short-answer responses?

6. How does knowing the mission and reviewing the strategic plan prepare you for a possible interview?

7. Does reviewing this plan increase or decrease your interest in the college?

8.3

Digesting Data

When you apply to a school you will not know everything about its admission process or priorities. And you'll have only a general idea about the rest of that year's applicant pool. But you are not completely in the dark either. You have the academic ranges that a school provides in its profile; you have last year's admit rate; and as we just covered in 8.1 and 8.2, you have indicators of its *mission* and *priorities*.

Now we are going to take a look at recent school-specific information that will provide you with additional insight through statistics, demographics, and trends. Known as the Common Data Set (CDS), this is standardized information colleges produce annually in order to "improve the quality and accuracy of information provided to all involved in a student's transition into higher education" (https://commondataset.org/). This can be a helpful tool for you as you are looking to understand the context around admission and enrollment numbers, beyond what is listed in schools' marketing materials or shared during presentations.

Combing through the CDS

Search online to find the most current year's CDS for a school you are interested in visiting, applying to, or attending. Section A will provide you a high-level overview of the institution, including whether it is private or public, coed or single-sex, as well as website and contact information.

Section B. Enrollment and persistence

What percentage of that institution is undergraduate versus graduate? What implications might that have for your experience on campus?

What percentage of the overall student enrollment does the first-year class constitute?

What percentage of their first-year class was men and what percentage was women? (*Bonus*: Look back over three to five years of data to determine if their gender balance is trending in one direction or the other.)

Note the number/percentage of students by ethnicity in the institution's first-year class and overall undergraduate population. What observations do you have about the diversity at this school? (*Bonus*: Look at the last three to five years of data to see if you can notice any trends.)

Find the data describing . . .

- four- and six-year graduation rates
- students receiving various forms of federal aid (Pell, Stafford, and so on)
- first-year retention rates

   You may want to create a table or document to compare various schools you are considering.

Section C. First-time, first-year (freshman) admission

- admit rate = total admits / total applicants
- yield rate = total enrolled / total admits

Does the admit rate or yield rate vary by gender?

Compare admit rates and/or gender data for several of the schools you are considering. Do you find any notable differences between schools?

Look back over several years of the CDS and identify any trends you see in application numbers and admit/yield rates.

Admission Factors

Continue exploring section C to understand the factors that each school uses in admission and the priority it places on each. As we discussed in chapter 7, you will find that highly selective schools incorporate far more factors beyond academics (extracurricular involvement, geographic origin, first-generation students, etc.). This section is a quantitative illustration of a nuanced holistic review that schools describe with lots of words on their websites and in recruiting presentations.

What can you learn in this section about the school(s) you are researching?

What questions might this information lead you to ask admission representatives from that school?

Are there data here that help you better understand your chances of admission or topics you might write about in response to that school's supplementary questions?

Testing

Later in section C you will be able to learn more about the role of testing in a college's admission process. You will find test score information by band for enrolled students. *Note*: Admitted averages are typically higher than enrolling averages, so you should assume the representation for admitted students in the higher bands is greater than these tables display. In other words, if 75+ percent of enrolling students scored above 600 on each section, it is likely their admitted pool was above 75 percent, and therefore the percentage of admitted students in the lower bands was lower than what the CDS lists.

Based on the information you find about testing, what additional questions do you have, and what implications might this have for you in application review?

What percentage of students at the schools you are considering fell into a test-score band similar to yours?

How does that information combined with your knowledge of a school's overall admit rate, as well as the composition of its class by gender, geography, ethnicity, and so on, inform whether that school is a reach, target, or likely school for you?

Class Rank

What percentage of students at the school you are researching finished in the top 10 percent of their class? _____. The top 20 percent? _____.

How do these data help you in understanding how competitive you might be for admission?

Early Action and Early Decision

If the college you are considering uses either or both early action and early decision, what is the admit rate in that round?

If you look back at a school's overall number of admits from earlier in section C, what percentage of its admits were given in early action or early decision?

What implications does this have, and what questions does this bring up, for you as you consider when and how to apply for admission?

There is a lot more information to find in the CDS, so we hope you will continue to explore each college you are considering, as well as to compare them with one another. This will also help you understand far more about how you may fit into a particular applicant pool than simply by looking at the information a school puts online. It should also help you refine your questions, apply to a balanced list of schools with varying admit rates, and home in on schools that put priority on your strengths.

8.4

Family Forward

In this chapter, we helped your student see how a college's mission state-ment and strategic plan are indicators of institutional priorities. In other words, everything we covered in chapters 6 and 7 concerned what colleges are looking at and for in applications, but how they make their admission decisions also hinges on what universities are attempting to become.

In order to help your student get a better sense of the demographic makeup of various colleges, as well as how those numbers break down in their applicant pool and admission process, we had them dig into Common Data Set (CDS). These are public, standardized data records that colleges pro-duce annually. Our intention is for students to understand from a quantita-tive standpoint the complexity of college admission decisions at universities employing holistic review.

Take a few minutes to search the CDS online for data from a school you want to learn more about or one you know your student has on their list at this point. You may want to compare the CDS from several schools to see how they differ or look over several years of data to note trends.

Section B is an excellent way to understand the composition of each col-lege, as well as persistence and graduation rates.

After reviewing this section, list three takeaways or questions:

1.

2.

3.

Section C brings numbers to much of what we covered in chapter 7. It describes the value colleges are placing or not placing on various aspects of holistic review, and it provides detailed information about GPA, class rank, and standardized testing.

After reviewing this section, list three takeaways or questions:

1.

2.

3.

Sections E and F focus on student life, campus culture, and various programs and offerings.

After reviewing these sections, list three takeaways or questions:

1.

2.

3.

Sections G and H display tuition and fee information, as well as scholarship and grant allocation.

After reviewing these section, list three takeaways or questions:

1.

2.

3.

Over the course of the last seven chapters, we have introduced you to a lot of aspects of college search and selection. Our hope is that you are continuing to keep an open mind and to focus more on *how* you and your family walk through this experience, rather than attempting to control or predict precisely *where* it all ends up.

8.5

Family Mission

In section 8.1, we asked your student to look at mission statements from a few colleges and write their own mission statement for their college admission experience. Our goal is to help them understand that just like companies have reasons for existing, so do schools. Schools make admission decisions in alignment with what they are attempting to accomplish or create, rather than simply admitting students based on who has the highest numbers.

Go online and read the mission statements for a few different colleges.

What differences do you notice?

What values or priorities do these colleges layout in their mission statement?

How do you think their mission might impact their review process or admission decisions?

Now that you have seen a number of mission statements from colleges, it is time to develop your own. If it helps, you could go check out the missions of some of your favorite brands or perhaps your own company or nonprofit.

Step 1. As a loving, supportive adult in this experience, start by writing words, phrases, or a sentence in response to these questions:

A. What are a few traits of the college you hope your student will select?

B. How do finances factor into your search and selection process?

C. What does success look like for you and your family in this experience?

D. How do relationships factor into the search for and decisions surrounding college?

Step 2. Review your answers and try to fill in the blanks here.

My mission in the college search, application and selection journey is to

_____

_____.

Along the way I am committed to _____

_____.

Ultimately I hope my student will attend a college that _____

_____.

When my student is in college and looks back at my role in their college admission journey, I hope they will say I was

_____

_____ .

Step 3. Now take ten to fifteen minutes to see if you can incorporate your answers from both steps into two or three sentences.

Step 4. Sleep on it. Take a day or two and then revisit your mission statement.

What is missing?

What edits, changes, deletions, or improvements can you make that encapsulate what you (not anyone else) are truly hoping for in this experience?

Feel free to continue to tinker with your mission statement. We will be asking you to share this in the Come Together section of this chapter.

8.6
Come Together

Students

We gave your family a chance to look into the CDS, but our prompts for them were not nearly as detailed as what we provided you.

Share a few of your observations and notes about specific schools:

- enrollment composition
- admission information
- graduation and retention rates

How might the CDS be a helpful tool as you visit, apply, or ultimately choose a school to attend?

What questions does the CDS bring up for you in general, or specific to the colleges you researched?

Parents

Discuss your notes from section 8.4 related to the CDS data you reviewed. *Explain* what you learned, discovered, or have questions about from sections G and H related to tuition, fees, grants, and scholarships.

How might you combine the CDS data with the information you got from the net price calculator in the money wedge part of chapter 3 (3.7)?

How might the CDS be a helpful tool for your family going forward in your search, application, and selection experience?

What questions does the CDS bring up for you in general or specifically about the colleges you researched?

Mission Statements

Take some time to share the mission statements you wrote earlier in this chapter.

1. What similarities do you see?

2. Discuss differences.

3. Overall, do your missions align given your separate roles and perspectives?

As a bonus, write a shared family mission statement.

Play Together

While it may not always feel this way to you, the truth is that YOU *control 75 percent of the college admission experience.*

- Of the thousands of schools in this country, you *decide* which ones you want to apply to. If you apply to seven colleges, you eliminate 99.9 percent of possible options. *You select where you apply.*

- As we have established, you *do not* control whether you are admitted or the amount of financial aid you receive. That part is out of your hands.

- At some point in your senior year, when you know what schools have admitted you, you will be able to look over your financial aid packages; revisit your goals, hopes, and dreams; listen to your parents' insight, advice, and encouragement; and make a choice.

- At this point, you own and control two-thirds of this exchange. We would argue there is a final piece too—*you* decide on your attitude, outlook, and approach once you arrive on campus too. Bam—75 percent! (With grade inflation, in some schools that is an A.)

While you are not going to be in the room where admission decisions are made, we want to help you understand what that feels like. So, for today, you are the admission committee. Take a look at the profile for "Good College." (Big thanks to our friends and colleagues Leah Lambert and Burke Rogers from the Asheville School for creating and sharing Good College with us all.)

Profile of Good College

Good College is a liberal arts college situated just outside Boston, Massachusetts, with an undergraduate enrollment of 4,100. Upon the heels of opening the new Sparkle Science Center and Laboratory complex, Good has just begun the first stage of a $125 million fund-raising campaign to enhance athletic facilities and build a new performing arts center.

Competing in NCAA Division III athletics, in the Super Liberal Arts College Conference, Good College allows for a true student-athlete experience. After a period of relative decline in athletic success, Good now hopes that enhanced facilities on campus will draw stronger student-athletes to bolster team success across the Athletic Department.

The president of Good College has recently reached out to alumni to kick off a fund-raising campaign. The president has also made it clear to the campus community and to the admissions office that enrolling a student body that reflects academic excellence and true diversity (ethnic, geographic, and socioeconomic) is of utmost importance and is at the heart of the college's mission.

Academic Profile of Admitted Good College Students, 2019–20:
Average GPA: 3.65 unweighted (A– overall) in very to most demanding coursework
Middle 50% ACT: 28–32   Middle 50% SAT (EBRW + M): 1350–1490

(Note: EBRW = evidence-based reading and writing; M = math)

Geographic Distribution of Student Body, 2019–20
New England: 30%   Mid-Atlantic: 22%
Southeast: 8%   Midwest: 11%
Mountain states: 3%   West Coast: 22%
International: 4%

Racial and Ethnic Diversity
White/Caucasian: 59%   Black/African American: 10%
Hispanic/Latino: 10%   Asian American/Pacific Islander: 5%
Native American: >1%   Decline to state/unknown: 16%

Given what you know now about institutional priorities and missions, what stands out to you about Good College's goals, and how could they impact admission decisions? To start working on yield and to compete with other colleges issuing their own decisions, your admission committee needs to get all admission decisions out tomorrow. After months of reading, your team has read all of the first-year applications and made notes. Now you are down to the final three students.

Read each student's summary and consider their ability to thrive academically and to match Good College's profile. We want each person on your committee to come up with an independent recommendation—*admit* one, *wait-list* one, and *deny* one—so do not confer with one another until you have all arrived at a recommendation.

Before you get started

- **GPAs** have been standardized on a **4.0 recalculated scale**.

- The **rigor of curriculum** was scored using this rubric:
    - **5** = Extremely challenging course selection in all subject areas. May have gone beyond school offerings to seek additional content.
    - **4** = Highly challenging course selection in all subject areas.
    - **3** = Moderately challenging course selection in most subject areas.
    - **2** = Less challenging course selection in some or most subject areas.
    - **1** = No evidence of rigorous course selection.

- Test scores have been superscored by combining the student's highest section subscores. *Good College is a test-optional school, so tests are not required for admission.*

- **Activities and extracurriculars** were scored according to this rubric:
    - **5** = *Extraordinary.* Made a major impact within school, community, or subject matter. An influencer either as a leader or independently. Sustained and purposeful activity over four years in three or more activities.
    - **4** = *Strong.* Strong involvement with some influence. Extreme depth in one to two areas or moderate depth in multiple areas. Sustained activity over three to four years.
    - **3** = *Solid.* Involved but lacking in influence. Busy but hasn't demonstrated growth in involvement. Involvement that isn't necessarily sustained but rather is pieced together over multiple years.

2 = *Average.* Sustained activity over two to three years. Has some gaps in involvement.

1 = *Lacking.* Minimal involvement. No sustained activity or evidence of influence.

The three applicant summaries are for Sara, Jenn, and Derek.

Name	Sara
High school, type	Evergreen High School, public
City, state	Bellevue, Washington
Gender	Female
Ethnicity	White
Context	Twin brother (not in our applicant pool)
Major	International affairs, Spanish
GPA	3.92
Rigor rating	4
Grade trends / academic notes	Top five in high school (187 in class)
Test scores	No testing scores submitted (not required at Good College)
Activities/extracurriculars	3; debate team all four years, job at local restaurant
Essay notes	On camping and hiking as a way she stays balanced. Insightful and introspective
Supplemental response notes	Discusses Good's science lab facilities and interdisciplinary interests
Teacher/counselor recommendation highlights	Academically focused
Interview	With Professor Abbott (international affairs): extremely bright and passionate about both Latin American history and politics. Fluent in Spanish and conversational in Portuguese
Visited campus / virtual program	Attended rocketry camp at Good after sophomore year
Discipline issues	Plagiarism and in-school suspension in ninth grade
Other notes	N/A

Name	Jenn
High school, type	Lone Star Country Day, private
City, state	Austin, Texas
Gender	Female
Ethnicity	Multiracial
Context	Parents married. Uncle is Good alum. Brother at University of Texas at Austin and sister a sophomore in high school
Major	Biology
GPA	3.83
Rigor rating	3
Grade trends / academic notes	Solid A−, B+ student. Strong senior schedule. Earned A in English 101 at the University of Texas last summer
Test scores	1410 SAT
Activities/extracurriculars	5; freelance web designer with clients in Austin, Houston, and Dallas. Student body vice president. Tennis, ranked in state
Essay notes	Strong writer. Humorous piece on family vacation in Chicago
Supplemental response	Wants to come to Good possibly for business. Likes Boston for internship opportunities and the business scene. History fanatic
Teacher/counselor recommendation highlights	Very well respected in school. Calm and confident. Known for being kind and self-assured
Interview	Allison Kipp, Good alum, in Texas: "polished and poised." Will take advantage of all Good has to offer if admitted
Visited campus / virtual program	Virtual info session and open house
Discipline issues	None
Other notes	Tennis coach interested. No scholarship but says she would definitely make the team

Name	Derek
High school	Massachusetts High School, public
City, state	Framingham, Massachusetts
Gender	Male
Ethnicity	Asian
Context	First generation, single parent
Major	Undecided
GPA	3.72
Rigor rating	4
Grade trends / academic notes	Rough freshman year but improving. Senior schedule includes Advance Placement physics and calculus and college English (dual enrollment)
Test scores	1360 SAT, 30 ACT
Activities/extracurriculars	4; helps with three younger siblings and at Mom's small business. Active in several school clubs. Lead actor in senior play
Essay notes	Compelling writer. Self-aware, mature, humble
Supplemental response notes	Discusses not feeling like Good College was a possibility for him until this year
Teacher/counselor recommendation highlights	Diligent, tenacious. Comes early to help ninth graders struggling in science. Quiet leader
Interview	Matt Thompson, admission team member: great conversation about Captain Marvel and recent project for Beta Club. Proud of his younger siblings and worried about leaving them
Visited campus / virtual program	Senior fall. Noted conversation with Dr. Katharine Keigh in bio
Discipline issues	No suspensions or expulsions
Other notes	Received email from principal last week advocating

Use the grid below to mark your vote, and discuss when everyone is done.

	Sara	Jenn	Derek
Admit			
Wait-list			
Deny			

1. What were the strengths and weaknesses of each student?

2. How did academic record factor into each decision?

3. What other contextual factors did you consider?

4. What would you like to have known more about each student?

5. How did Good College's goals and mission factor into your decisions?

6. Whom did you admit, deny, and wait-list and why?

7. Students, how does working through this exercise impact your perspective on admission decisions?

8. Parents, how does working through this exercise impact your perspective on admission decisions and your role in the admission experience?

Stay Together

Handling admission decisions. Now that you have seen firsthand how institutional priorities and mission impact college admission, we hope you understand that while decisions feel personal, they are not. This is a critical lesson to remember: selective colleges deny, defer, and wait-list students (thousands of them) who they not only believe can be academically successful on their campus but whom they also admire for their character, achievements, and potential.

Now everybody go to your room. Sorry; that sounded harsh. Please go to your room and get every pair of shoes you own. Meet back in the living room in ten minutes. (Don't forget to check the front closet and back porch.) We want everyone to imagine you are going on a forty-five-mile walk. Pick the pair of shoes that best "fits" given your mission and put them on. Tell you what: you can put one other pair in your backpack in case of rain.

Parents answer these questions first, followed by the student:

Why did you pick those shoes?

Are they the most expensive pair you have?

Are they the prettiest or the newest?

Now imagine you can take two people with you on this walk. Who comes to mind? Think about friends, family members, classmates, actors, athletes, or even people from history. The only catch is this: if they can't walk the entire way, you have to start over at mile one.

Whom are you going to choose and why?

Whom would you want to bring if it were not for that whole start-over thing?

TRANSLATION: If you are applying to a college taking less than 50 percent of applicants, you need to understand that many students who are not admitted are smart, talented, and bound for future success. To put it in terms of our shoe analogy, if the assignment had been to pick shoes for a wedding, we are guessing you would have picked differently. In a selective review process, getting edged out for reasons you may never know is a distinct possibility. As our friend Pam Ambler, associate director of college counseling at Pace Academy in Atlanta, says, "The way that admission decisions *feel* is not how they are *made*."

BOTTOM LINE: You may be the smartest, nicest, most promising student in your high school, county, or even state, but in that year, for that college, based on where you're from or what you want to study or what that college is emphasizing or deemphasizing (institutional priorities)—plus the competition in the applicant pool, of course—you may not get admitted.

Students, maybe one day highly selective colleges will put a checkbox on their application asking students to acknowledge that they understand they are entering a process that is not quantifiable or fair. Until that time, we have developed a pledge for you to sign (first pledge below) before you submit your applications. Likewise, **family members**, we have developed a pledge for you to sign (second one below) during the admission experience.

Pledges for the admission experience

I, _____, *being of sound (though overly caffeinated) mind and (sleep-deprived) body, do hereby swear not to presume anything in a selective or holistic admission process. I will not expect my test scores or my grades in high school, regardless of their quality, to guarantee my admittance. I understand holistic admission is neither fair nor perfect and thus will not waste my senior year attempting to predict results, second-guessing myself, or concerning myself with what I cannot control. Furthermore, I agree not to view an admission denial as an indictment of my character, a judgment on my preparation, or a prediction of my future success.*

Signature _____ Date _____

I, _____, *understand my role is to support, coach, partner, and guide my student. Therefore and henceforth, I will use pronouns singular in number ("I" not "we") when referring to college hopes and dreams. I vow not to emulate the voice of my student or hack their email or portal account so that I can do for them what they need to do for themselves in their college admission experience. I promise not to begrudge the joy and excitement of my friends when their children receive acceptances, and I commit to celebrating every offer of admission my student receives. Furthermore, I agree not to view admission decisions as validation of my success as a parent but rather as a reminder of the temporary versus the permanent.*

Signature _____ Date _____

Want to put your own spin on a pledge? Go for it. Regardless of whether you accept the pledges above or write your own, we want you to sign your pledge before the first application gets submitted.

Chapter 9

Making Your College Choice

Congratulations! By the time you get to this chapter, you have accomplished your goal of having offers of admission from several colleges. Do not rush past that and begin to stress now about making a decision. Take the time to celebrate and reflect on all it has taken you to get here. As you come down the home stretch of your college admission experience, we hope you are feeling excited and confident. If you have taken advantage of the exercises in this book and have done the work, now you just need to apply what you have learned about yourself and the schools to which you have been accepted in order to make a final decision. Easy, right?

Not for everyone. For some, this is the most significant decision they have ever made. First and foremost, it is critical for you to realize that there is no right choice. Your college experience will not be perfect, and there is no one school that will meet all your needs. If you can approach your decision with that mindset, it will help you relax and move forward. This chapter is designed to provide you with valuable activities and resources to support you in making *your* final decision. Don't take shortcuts or settle for easy answers—dig deep and have confidence in your exploration and ultimate choice.

With the colleges lucky enough to make your short list, you are in the driver's seat now, so take each college you are considering for a spin. Attend the formal admitted student programs that each school offers, and also do your own informal review by soliciting different perspectives and gathering the information you need to know to make an informed decision. Before you revisit schools, take some time to return to the exercises you completed earlier in the book. Read over your self-reflection, review your needs and wants, and look back at how the funnel of your search narrowed to where it is today. What has changed, and what remains constant? A lot can happen in a year, and while your values may be the same, your interests or hopes for your future might have shifted. This is to be expected. Frankly, we would be concerned if you have not grown or discovered new areas of interest in the past twelve months. Maybe family finances or dynamics have changed, and this will impact where you go to college. Just because you were "all in" at one school when you applied, doesn't mean you have to stick to that. Remember the ego that we addressed in chapter 3? Keep it in check, and make sure you are not ceding your control to others or to your pride.

Here is the thing. Nobody else can make this decision for you. While that can feel like a burden, it's really a huge privilege. Our hope is you won't feel like you *have* to do this but you *get* to do this. Own it and celebrate it. Great opportunity lies ahead. Trust your gut. It may not seem like it in the moment, but the truth is you cannot go wrong.

9.1

Student Decision History

Before you make your college choice, take some time to consider other decisions you have made in the past.

Decision 1

What steps did you take to decide?

What information did you need to gather, and how did you do it?

Whom did you involve, if anyone, in the decision-making process?

Were you pleased with your decision?

What, if anything, would you do differently now?

Decision 2

What steps did you take to decide?

What information did you need to gather, and how did you do it?

Whom did you involve, if anyone, in the decision-making process?

Were you pleased with your decision?

What, if anything, would you do differently now?

9.2

Checking on Change

In the early chapters of this book and in your college search, you invested significant time and energy into identifying your *why*: what you value and are interested in and the experience you hope to have in college. That was likely a while ago, and inevitably you and circumstances have changed. Maybe this does not impact your college decision, but it is still helpful to reflect on this evolution. Answer the questions below. (You may find it helpful to refer to exercises you completed in the first half of the book to jog your memory.)

What big developments in your life, family, school, community, and world have taken place over the past year?

List five to ten criteria or needs and wants you had for a college when you began your search, and cross out any that are no longer true.

List five to ten college characteristics that you didn't know you wanted when you built your list but now know are desirable.

How do your answers to three questions above impact your college decision?

==================== **9.3** ====================

Financial Factors

Unfortunately, financial aid award letters all look different. Our friend and colleague John Leach, associate vice provost for enrollment and university financial aid at Emory University, uses an illustration in presentations to families to help them see how costs may compare at different kinds of institutions. The abbreviation EFC in the illustration stands for *expected family contribution*, which is the amount that a family plans to cover of a year's worth (in this case) of college costs.

What might a sample aid package look like?

	Selective private	Other private	Public university
Cost of attendance	$72,000	$42,000	$19,000
Family contribution (calculated EFC)	$15,000	$15,000	$15,000
Financial need	$57,000	$27,000	$4,000
Merit scholarship	$3,500	$8,000	$0
Need–based grant	$51,000	$2,700	$0
Student loan	$0	$5,500	$3,500
Work Study	$2,500	$1,800	$0
Total aid	$57,000	$18,000	$3,500
Unmet need ("gap")	$0	$9,000	$500
Total paid	$15,000	$24,000+loan +interest	$15,500+loan +interest

Create your own spreadsheet or use the one below to assess your financial aid offers in a uniform manner and to understand the real costs of earning a college degree at each of the schools you are considering. This financial decision spreadsheet will allow you to have transparent conversations and open discussions about the implications for your family and future.

College		
Total cost of attendance		
Federal grant		
Institutional grant		
Institutional scholarship		
Other scholarship		
Total grant and scholarship aid		
Subsidized student loan		
Unsubsidized student loan		
Federal Perkins loan		
Parent loan		
Other loan		
Federal Work-Study		
Total loan offer		
Total financial aid offer		
Cost to you		

9.4

Pros and Cons

Once you have narrowed your choices to two or three schools, it is time to highlight the strengths of each school and the aspects you wish were different. Use the following table to record the pros and cons of each school so that you can see them side by side.

COLLEGE			
PROS			
CONS			

9.5

All In

One of the best ways to test a decision is to live with it. That is why some automobile dealers allow buyers to take a car home for a week. Even mattress companies let you sleep on your new purchase for a few nights without penalty for return. While this is not as easy with choosing a college, you can replicate this tryout experience to an extent.

The Activity

Once you have narrowed your choices, spend a few days imagining you have chosen each school. Tell yourself that you have enrolled at that college, and do your best to put your other options out of your mind. If you have a sweatshirt, hat, mug or other gear from that college, wear, use it, and live it. Visit the college's website each day to see what news gets posted and what is happening on campus. Check out the social media feeds from the college and enrolled students. After going "all in," complete the reflection below. Repeat this exercise for the other colleges you are seriously considering.

The Reflection

This part is perhaps the most important aspect of the exercise, so save it until the end of your time considering each school.

1. What is your gut reaction?

2. What made you excited?

3. What reservations or feelings of regret did you have throughout the week?

4. Did anything specific make you feel uncomfortable?

5. What were you missing if anything?

9.6

Revisit

One of the best ways to help you decide on a college is to attend the accepted student programs. Whether in-person or virtual, these events are colleges' opportunity to convince you to accept their admission offer, and they will likely try to do so with great fanfare. You will be exposed to many areas of campus life, but bear in mind that it will be what *they* want you to see.

Use this form to write down the information you still need and the questions that linger. You might have general questions about student culture or the school's relationship with the surrounding town, or your questions might be specifically about support for student mental health or special academic programs. Record your answers during or soon after each accepted student program.

QUESTION	ANSWER

9.7

Reflect

The questions below will help you make sense of all the information you took in through your research or during accepted student programs. Ideally you have now been able to connect with a diverse range of students, faculty, and staff and have attended informational programs and asked directed questions. Now, for each college you are considering, reflect on the following and make notes for yourself.

Will You Feel Comfortable?

Food

- Does the meal plan allow for flexibility, or is it limited in choice?

- Are you required to carry the school's meal plan in your first year only or throughout your entire time on campus?

- Are there spaces where you can cook for yourself?

- Are there gluten-free, kosher, or nondairy options?

- Are there local grocery stores and restaurants that provide food options to supplement campus offerings?

Housing

- Are there substance-free housing options if this is a priority for you?

- Are single-gender floors or residence halls available?

- Is there gender-expansive or gender-nonconforming housing or bathrooms?

- Can first-year students have single rooms, or are double rooms, suites, triples, or apartment-style setups the standard?

Will You Feel Safe and Welcome?

Physical safety

- What systems are in place for campus alerts or emergency notification? How are parents made aware of crime or other incidents that occur on campus?

- What was the highest-profile crime reported on campus in the past year? How does that compare with other schools you are considering, other colleges in the area, and your city or hometown?

- How safe is the neighborhood surrounding campus?

- What is the relationship like between the college and the town?

- What are the campus statistics for reports of dating violence, domestic violence, sexual assault, and stalking?

- What procedures exist for institutional disciplinary action in cases of dating violence, domestic violence, sexual assault, stalking, and other crimes?

- Does campus security provide a safe escort service in the evening, and if so, how accessible is it and how often is it used?

Intellectual safety

- What is the academic climate on campus like?

- How supportive is the campus community toward freedom of expression (inside and outside the classroom)?

- Are students and faculty open to diverse opinions and perspectives? Do they "talk across the aisle"?

- Has the campus hosted controversial speakers, and what was the community's response?

- What is the academic culture around "trigger warnings"?

Will you belong?

- Who are the types of people that challenge, support, stretch, and encourage you?

- What types of individuals do you like to surround yourself with?

- Are you looking for a college experience that mirrors your home or high school or one that takes you outside your comfort zone and exposes you to a new and different culture?

- Do you want a college that has a lot of school spirit?

- Are students engaged in and out of class?

- What do students do on weekends?

- Is it a "suitcase campus" where students tend to go their separate ways when classes are done?

- How connected are the alumni? Is there a strong network that persists beyond the campus gates?

- Do you feel a sense of community, connection, and belonging on campus?

- If you are honest with yourself, do you really see yourself there?

Can you be successful?

- In the past, what experiences and environments have provided you with the encouragement and inspiration to grow?

- Will the culture, faculty, and fellow students at the school offer the freedom you need to be proud of your accomplishments and to both discover and enhance your talents and abilities?

- In college, do you want to be a big fish in a small pond or a small fish in a big pond?

- Do you sense this is a place where you will spend your time feeling like you don't measure up, or is it a place that will inspire you to find confidence in your potential to excel?

- Will you grow at the school?

- Can you identify three specific ways you're excited to make community and make your mark there?

Can you thrive?

- Will this college allow you to be your best self?

- As you consider college options, what resources and supports exist on each campus to help you reach your goals?

- Are you interested in double majoring or pursuing a minor? If so, how flexible is the curriculum?

- Do you want the ability to delve immediately into your major, or do you want a school that provides the breadth and depth of offerings necessary to allow for exploration?

9.8

Family Forward

Raising children is full of milestones. First words, first steps, first day of school, first time driving a car—the list goes on and on. It is a parental instinct to want to protect our children and do everything we can to ensure their happiness and success. We held them up as they attempted to walk and applied the imaginary brake as they learned to drive (as we gripped everything in sight with white knuckles). Now comes another significant moment of transition, one that can often be layered with complicated feelings of excitement, fear, and an urge to control.

You have had over a decade of practice, and it is game day. Throughout this book we have tried to help you scaffold the experience of searching for and applying to college with your child. If you have done the exercises and had the important conversations at each step, the process of making a decision should be manageable. (Notice that we did not say *easy*.)

It is going to be tempting for you to provide answers as your child tries to decide on the school that is the best match for them. Resist. Your job continues to be that of a coach, not a player. Trust that you have provided them with the resources and practice they need to own this experience of discernment. Yes, in many ways, this remains a family decision, as finances and other factors will impact you all. Exercise 9.10 will help you and your student consider the role that return on investment might play in the decision. However, if your student doesn't take the lead in the final choice, they will not be invested in the outcome in the ways they will need to be in order to succeed in college and beyond.

The best thing you can do now is listen and be a sounding board that reflects what you hear from them. You will see things in them that they might not see in themselves, and you will need to walk a fine line between bringing that to light and burdening them with your opinions and preferences. Your job is to ask questions and then help your child process their own answers, not provide them. Offer them support and resources, and then step back and let them be self- advocates. And perhaps most importantly, again, just listen.

In this chapter we have provided tools for students when considering their options and how they will make decisions. These will be critical skills for them to employ in college when you are not down the hall. Take deep breaths, and have faith in how you have raised them.

9.9

Family Decision History

As your student makes their college choice, take some time to consider significant decisions you have made in your life.

Decision 1

What steps did you take to decide?

What information did you need to gather, and how did you do it?

Whom did you involve, if anyone, in the decision-making process?

Were you pleased with your decision?

What, if anything, would you do differently now?

Decision 2

What steps did you take to decide?

What information did you need to gather, and how did you do it?

Whom did you involve, if anyone, in the decision-making process?

Were you pleased with your decision?

What, if anything, would you do differently now?

9.10

Investigating Investment

Our friend and colleague Shereem Herndon-Brown, founder and director of Strategic Admissions Advice (www.strategicadmissionsadvice.com), encourages families to consider the

significant investment they are making in a number of ways. The recommendations in this section are adapted from his guidance.

With college costs ranging from $25K to $75K annually, a natural question for any parent to ask is, What will be the return on investment (ROI) for my kid's college education? To calculate ROI, total a student's earnings for ten years after graduation and divide that total by the cost of their college education. The higher the ROI, the better a financial bet the school is, on average. As you weigh your family's choice of college, your job is to weigh both the actual costs and the potential ROI.

Prior to making a choice, make sure you have compared these features of the colleges:

- total cost

- projected debt (if any)

- graduation rates (four-year, five-year, six-year)

- co-op or internship opportunities and wages

- job placement rates and mid-career earnings by major

- loan default rates of recent graduates, ideally by major

- career services and job placement efforts at the college

Other Considerations

Funding a college education can feel overwhelming due to varying costs, nonstandardized aid packages, and short-term versus long-term realities and speculation. As hard as it may be, do not take it personally if a college that you want your child to attend does not offer what you believe you need or they deserve financially.

Our hope is that you took our advice in chapter 3 and clearly laid out conditions, expectations, and limitations in choosing a certain college or major. If that is not the case, now is the time to be abundantly clear about this final choice and how your ROI factors into that decision.

Tools to Evaluate ROI

College Navigator provides insight into a school's graduation, job placement, and student loan default rates (https://nces.ed.gov/collegenavigator/).

College Scorecard provides information on how much money a school's graduates earn, how much student loan debt they carry on average, and how many graduates keep their loans in good standing (https://collegescorecard.ed.gov/).

Occupational Outlook Handbook provides information on different jobs, projected growth, median salaries, and necessary education (https://www.bls.gov/ooh/home.htm).

Use the table below to compare the colleges on a student's short list. Based on the information you gathered from the sources above and your own research, assign each college an ROI score from 1 (poor ROI) to 10 (excellent ROI).

College			
Annual cost to your family			
Median annual earnings of students 2 years after graduation			
4-year graduation rate			
Projected total debt after 4 years (if any)			
Other notes			

9.11

Come Together

Arguably, this is the most important Come Together discussion yet. Before you move ahead in your conversations about a final college choice, be sure you have taken time as a family to hit pause and celebrate the successes so far and the privilege of having choices. Remember that you don't *have* to do this; you *get* to do this. It is easy to feel the weight of needing to make a decision, but this is an exciting time to consider future opportunities. Don't lose sight of that.

Pause for Praise

First things first. Before you begin, take a moment to let everyone share at least one thing you appreciate about each other. What are you grateful for? It might be a comment made along the way or an observation about how a family member approached the experience. What stands out, and why are you thankful?

Decision Debrief

We have asked both students and parents to complete the decision history exercise (9.1 and 9.9). Share your responses, and talk about the different ways you have made decisions in the past and what you learned. Reflect together on how these lessons might inform the decision in front of you.

Student Summary

Students, share your responses to the exercises that we asked you to complete. You've likely done this along the way as you revisited schools, but after you have completed all of the accepted student programs, discuss your reflections with your family members. Also walk them through the pros and cons worksheet and your experience with the "all in" exercise.

What do you need from your family members? Be as clear as possible about how they can support you right now. Do you want feedback and input? Or are you just looking for a listening ear? What role are you hoping your parents will play in your college decision?

Parent and Family Playback

Parents, reflect back to your student what you are hearing about how you can be supportive. Share how you are feeling about their decision-making process, and reinforce your trust in them. Offer to provide whatever resources you can to help them in their final decision. Remind them that life is not linear and that they will make the best decision for themselves in this moment. Be straightforward about any concerns you have, and don't let important pieces go unsaid.

Choose and Celebrate

Before you close out this final Come Together, have a conversation about how, when, and where to share the exciting news—and importantly who will share it. Too often we have seen parents' pride or excitement cause them to jump the gun and post on social media before the student has had a chance to tell friends and family. After all you that have worked through to get to this point, be sure you are on the same page.

Now for the really fun part. Pick something special or sentimental, and go celebrate as a family!

9.12

Next Steps

Once your family has come to a joint decision (and you have celebrated), there are a few final practical matters to take care of.

1. **Hold Your Spot**. Go online to your admission portal and either complete the "intent to enroll form" and/or pay your admission deposit. If you are financially unable to pay the deposit, you should reach out to the admission or financial aid office to discuss a waiver or other options. Although you would be in good company if you waited until midnight of deposit day to pay, we hope you will commit before that. Life lesson: deadline means DEADline.

2. **Close Other Doors**. Many students simply ghost the colleges they decide not to attend. We hope we have talked enough about character, integrity, and responsibility in this book that you will not be one of them. Once you have held your spot at your college of choice, cancel your applications at the other schools that offered you admission, either through your admission portal or by sending the admission office an email thanking them for the opportunity and declining the offer. This may let the office give your spot to another student, and it will end the emails or texts the office is sending you.

3. **Go All In**. Sound familiar? The "all in" exercise (9.5) was just the preview. This is the real deal. Go online or visit campus and buy a school t-shirt, put a decal on the car window, start following student groups on social media, and donate or trade the shirts you have from other schools.

Michael Schell, director of college counseling at Catholic Memorial School tells students, "Guard yourself from the temptation to think the grass is greener elsewhere. Begin your conversations with others and within yourself with an attitude of gratitude for the opportunities you have rather than a spirit of entitlement or loss."

Chapter 10

Closing Letters

In the age of text, email, and instant message, writing personal letters is in many ways a lost art. When was the last time you received a handwritten letter or sent a personal note? You probably can't remember. I (Brennan) started a tradition when my kids were young that was inspired by my long-time college counseling colleague, Bruce Berk. Every year on my kids' birthdays, I write them a personal letter (please note this is not in lieu of gifts ... I don't want a mutiny on my hands). In their letters, I document the past year and the many ways they have grown. I write about the challenges they faced, the strengths they developed, and the adventures they had.

Year by year, I am chronicling the first chapters of their lives, expressing how much I love them and relaying the myriad ways I am proud of them. These are important moments of transition that provide the opportunity to pause and reflect. Along with the notes, I include an array of photos from the year and give the letter to my son or daughter as we celebrate their birthday. It has been incredibly gratifying to see that as they have become teenagers, they actually anticipate my notes more than any gift. They dive right into reading the letter in front of me and then we spend time talking, laughing, and reminiscing about the past twelve months. It has become such a meaningful tradition that in recent years, totally on their own initiative, they have begun doing the same on my birthday.

We are not necessarily suggesting you adopt this tradition (though it is never too late to start), but we are asking that you, as you conclude the admission experience, engage in a similar exercise—students writing a letter to parents and parents doing the same. Although we provide a general structure to help guide you and frame these letters, we hope you will make them your own. As we have said throughout this book, the college admission experience is an opportunity to reflect, encourage, learn, and grow closer as a family.

Don't skip this final step. Too often families go through this whole search, application, and decision experience and then immediately move on without taking the time to pause and celebrate together. Use these letters to express that journey, growth, and discovery.

10.1

Student Letter to Parents

Okay, students, here we go. Remember those cards for birthdays, Father's Day, Mother's Day, and the winter holidays that you used to make for your parents as a younger kid? Inevitably they included creative pictures with disproportionate bodies, barely legible handwriting, reversed letters or numbers, and at least one misspelling—sometimes of your own name or theirs. They were colorful, busy, and unique. The reason your parents kept and treasured them was not because they were perfect but because they were deeply personal—because of the thought and effort you put into creating them. This is the grownup version.

Write a letter—not a text, not an email, not a shoutout on Instagram—to your parents. Yes, this will require multisyllabic words and ideally multiple paragraphs, but every sentence will go a long way. There are only two phrases that should each appear at least once in your letter: "I love you!" and "Thank you." The rest is up to you.

The questions suggested below are just prompts to get you thinking about what you might include. Ultimately, we hope your letter will be as creative, colorful, and personal as the birthday cards that you gave your parents when you were little. Remember to write from the heart.

- What has been memorable about this admission experience?

- How have you grown in the past year and what was their role in that?

- What were the ways that you felt most supported by your parents?

- What are you looking forward to most in college?

- What specifically are you grateful for?

- What is one thing you have never said to your parents but have always wanted to?

- What do you value about your relationship with your parents?

- What do you love about them?

- What else do you want to make sure they know?

10.2

Family (Parents) Letter to Student

Before we get into your assignment let us first say, *thank you.*

Thank you for taking the time to read through—and work through—this workbook. Thank you for your time, your energy, and most of all for loving your kids. Thank you for consistently encouraging them and faithfully supporting them. Thank you for advocating for them. Thank you for wanting them to have a better life and more opportunities and experiences than you have had.

Thank you for washing the same dishes and clothes a thousand times. Thank you for driving to and from practice and sitting through hours of swim meets or dance or music performances (just to hear or see your child perform for a fraction of that time).

As parents, whether our kids are 7, 17, or 37 years old, we never stop trying to lift them up. Whether they say it or not (and we have told them to), they love and appreciate you. We know you are not perfect (we certainly are not), but you are committed to them. And for that, we truly *thank* you!

Last year I (Rick) was reorganizing our pantry. This is something I do regularly. I confess it's a bit neurotic, but it makes me feel better. Anyway, deep in the back corner I found a soft-cover lunch bag my son had used in the

fourth grade. Before I threw it out, I unzipped the front pocket to find close to eighty handwritten notes I had put in his lunches that year. Some of them were more creative or specific than others, but the fact that he kept them . . . well, let's just say it must have been really dusty in the pantry that day.

We understand that their occasional eye rolls or mumbled one-syllable responses or intentional button-pushing may be an odd way of showing it, but the truth is your kids love you. While they may talk a big game about heading off to college or what they want life to look like when they are no longer at home, they need you. And after watching the admission cycle repeat itself for two decades now, I am convinced that they specifically need to hear three things from you:

1. You love them.

2. You trust them.

3. You are proud of them.

For this final exercise, we want you to write your child a letter. Now, you can put those three sentiments in your own order, language, and style, but the nonnegotiable is that all three *must* be included.

Here are some questions to consider as you gather your thoughts and begin to work on your letter. And to finish where I started (and in advance and on behalf of your student), THANK YOU!

- What has been memorable about this admission experience?
- How have you grown closer as a family during this time, and what was your student's role in that?
- What about them are you especially proud of?
- What have they taught you?
- What will you most miss about having them around day-to-day when they go to college?
- What specifically are you grateful for?
- What is one thing you have never said to your child but have always wanted to?
- What do you value about your relationship?
- What do you love about them?
- What else do you want to make sure they know?

Afterword

We have come to appreciate that coauthoring a book has many parallels with a family going through the college search and admission experience. While most people only see the end result, a lot of work, energy, compromise, and collaboration has to take place along the way to be successful.

When we set out to collaborate, we were confident we had the same goal and a very similar message—keep perspective, breathe, and control what we can control. We knew, however, that our styles, backgrounds, and approaches varied. Brennan writes regularly for Forbes.com and other esteemed outlets and works on serious research at the Harvard Graduate School of Education. Meanwhile, Rick writes a college admission blog.

Inevitably, if Rick had written this workbook on his own, it would have been very college focused. Brennan's rich experience teaching and working with students and families on the high school side, and his ability to ask good questions, pushed Rick to communicate more clearly and to think carefully about how to articulate parts of the admission work that can seem mysterious or unclear to those on the outside looking in. The depth of Rick's experience with the admission landscape, enrollment pressures, and other intricacies of the field, along with his refreshingly transparent and relaxed approach, provided Brennan perspective and ease.

Along the way, we both gave ground (for Rick, that primarily meant fewer sarcastic parentheticals and obscure movie references; for Brennan, that meant fewer words) and stood our ground. We continually worked to find the balance of encouraging each other, holding each other accountable, and editing each other's writing with equal measures of confidence and grace.

In the end, this workbook truly was a shared effort that merged the best of our different insights and backgrounds. Importantly, it also served to further solidify our trust and friendship. As we said in this workbook, and also in *The Truth about College Admission*, that is our wish for your family as well: that your college search will be a unifying experience. We hope that, like the actual college experience, the admission experience will be an opportunity to grow closer, learn about yourself and those around you, seek a multitude of perspectives, and really listen; that you will worry less about unheard conversations in committee rooms hundreds of miles away and instead will focus on clear and compassionate discussions in the rooms you walk into every day.

Thank you for reading and working through this workbook together, and with us. We are truly honored.

Acknowledgments

We are grateful for the many students, families, counselors, and friends who have provided such valuable feedback since the 2019 release of *The Truth about College Admission: A Family Guide to Getting In and Staying Together*. It was your encouragement and support that led to this workbook and inspired us to consider how we could bring our words to practice. Thanks to the exceptional educators who contributed their wisdom and resources to this workbook: Susan Tree, Shereem Herndon-Brown, Allison Matlack, John Leach, Cicily Shaw, Michael Schell, Diane Campbell, Brian Smith, Danny Easley, Meg Scheid, Jeff Kurtzman, Michael Trivette, Todd Rinehart, and Bruce Berk.

Finally, we are fortunate to have such a supportive and joyful editor in Greg Britton. He and the team at Johns Hopkins University Press have continually encouraged and believed in us, our mission, and the potential of this resource for families and schools.

BRENNAN

To my children, Samuel and Rebecca. You make me a better person, father, and educator. You have been wonderfully giving of your time and love, and your support of my many endeavors means the world to me. I am inspired by your ability to live in the moment with joy and I am uplifted by your laughs and deep thoughtfulness. To my father, Timothy. Your selfless care for family, friends, community, the environment, and the well-being of our world is something I aspire to. I hope to be the father and professional you have modeled, and your ability to say the right thing at the right time is enviable. To my mother, Marjorie, whom we miss every day. Your love and insight made me who I am, and your compassionate work as a counselor is my guiding light. To my siblings, their families, and Meredy. I am grateful for your encouragement, and I am blessed to have such a supportive family. I am also thankful for my exceptional colleagues and friends at The Derryfield School and Making Caring Common, whose dedication to young people and to creating a better world makes me feel hopeful. I am especially lucky to have a great team in Amanda Gagne and Jill Teeters, who provide such helpful feedback and support. I am also grateful for the individuals and networks that make up the Character Collaborative, Clam Nation, and US Performance Academy as well as the many amazing educators of ACCIS, NACAC/NEACAC, and LRISCCA. You make this a great profession and remind me why I do what I do. To my close friends. You know who you are. Our walks, talks, adventures, and connections have sustained me and brought joy to my life in both good and challenging times. Thank you and love to you.

RICK

To my ridiculously patient and beautiful wife, Amy, who models every day the person I want to be someday. My kids, Andrew and Elizabeth, for the reminder that the most important things in life are simple and for bringing ineffable joy, purpose, and pride. Beyond thankful for my parents and sister for instilling confidence and demonstrating unconditional love. To the leadership of Georgia Tech for giving me the space to innovate, create, and risk in the name of Progress and Service. Inexpressible appreciation and respect to my long-time colleagues for their constant encouragement and support, especially Matt McLendon, Mary Tipton Woolley, Katie Faussemagne, Paul Kohn, Deborah Smith, Becky Tankersley, George P. Burdell, and the unbelievably talented, passionate, and committed teams I've had the chance to serve alongside. Go Jackets! WSTE. Leadership Georgia for reminding me "we get to do this." To the All Souls congregation for years of care and community. Cheers to Clambake Nation ("Hi, Neighbor!"). Lastly, a huge shoutout and mad props to the NACAC/SACAC family for inspiring me to speak, write, and lead in the name of students, access, educational progress, and equity. Finally, my brothers Terry, Crewser, and the McCauley Street boys, who share a bond unbroken by time or place. Much love.

Resources to Read-Listen-Watch-Explore

Books

Anxious Kids Anxious Parents: 7 Ways to Stop the Worry Cycle and Raise Courageous and Independent Children by Lynn Lyons and Reid Wilson (2013)

At What Cost? Defending Adolescent Development in Fiercely Competitive Schools by David L. Gleason, PsyD (2017)

Better Decisions, Fewer Regrets by Andy Stanley (2020)

Colleges That Change Lives: 40 Schools That Will Change the Way You Think about Colleges by Loren Pope (2012)

College: What It Was, Is, and Should Be by Andrew Delbanco (2014)

Creating a Class: College Admissions and the Education of Elites by Mitchell Stevens (2007)

David & Goliath: Underdogs, Misfits, and the Art of Battling Giants by Malcolm Gladwell (2015)

Excellent Sheep: The Miseducation of the American Elite and the Way to a Meaningful Life by William Deresiewicz (2015)

Far from the Tree: Parents, Children, and the Search for Identity by Andrew Solomon (2012)

Fiske Guide to Colleges 2019 by Edward B. Fiske (2019)

The Gift of Failure: How the Best Parents Learn to Let Go So Their Children Can Succeed by Jessica Lahey (2016)

Give and Take: Why Helping Others Drives Our Success by Adam Grant (2013)

Grit: The Power of Passion and Perseverance by Angela Duckworth (2016)

How Children Succeed: Grit, Curiosity, and the Power of Character by Paul Tough (2012)

How to Raise an Adult: Break Free of the Overparenting Trap and Prepare Your Kid for Success by Julie Lythcott-Haims (2015)

Know What You're FOR: A Growth Strategy for Work, an Even Better Strategy for Life by Jeff Henderson (2019)

Letting Go: A Parents' Guide to Understanding the College Years, sixth edition, by Karen Levin Coburn (2016)

Let Your Life Speak: Listening for the Voice of Vocation by Parker Palmer (1999)

The Naked Roommate: And 107 Other Issues You Might Run into in College by Harlan Cohen (2017)

The Overachievers: The Secret Lives of Driven Kids by Alexandra Robbins (2006)

The Paradox of Choice: Why More Is Less by Barry Schwartz (2004)

The Parents We Mean to Be: How Well-Intentioned Adults Undermine Children's Moral and Emotional Development by Richard Weissbourd (2010)

Pressured Parents, Stressed-Out Kids by Wendy S. Grolnick, PhD, and Kathy Seal (2008)

The Price You Pay for College: An Entirely New Road Map for the Biggest Financial Decision Your Family Will Ever Make by Ron Lieber (2020)

The Road to Character by David Brooks (2016)

Start with Why: How Great Leaders Inspire Everyone to Take Action by Simon Sinek (2009)

The Teenage Brain: A Neuroscientist's Survival Guide to Raising Adolescents and Young Adults by Frances E. Jensen and Amy Ellis Nutt (2015)

There Is Life after College: What Parents and Students Should Know about Navigating School to Prepare for the Jobs of Tomorrow by Jeffrey J. Selingo (2017)

Where You Go Is Not Who You'll Be: An Antidote to the College Admissions Mania by Frank Bruni (2016)

Who Gets In and Why: A Year Inside College Admissions by Jeffrey J. Selingo (2020)

The Years That Matter Most: How College Makes or Breaks Us by Paul Tough (2019)

Articles and Blogs

https://jonboeckenstedt.net/higher-ed-data-stories/

https://mandywallace.com/the-art-of-brevity-5-powerful-techniques-to-cut-the-fluff-from-your-fiction/

https://mcc.gse.harvard.edu/reports/turning-the-tide-college-admissions

https://mcc.gse.harvard.edu/resources-for-families/ethical-parenting-in-the-college-admissions-process

https://mcc.gse.harvard.edu/resources-for-families/red-flags-for-parentsare
-you-putting-too-much-pressure-on-your-child-during-the-college
-admission-process

https://sites.gatech.edu/admission-blog/

https://www.collegeessayguy.com/blog

https://www.forbes.com/sites/akilbello/

https://www.forbes.com/sites/brennanbarnard/

https://www.tuitionfit.org/in-the-college-search-roi-and-fit-have-to-go
-hand-in-hand/

WATCH THIS

- Barry Schwartz Paradox of Choice Ted Talk: https://www.ted.com/talks
/barry_schwartz_the_paradox_of_choice?language=en

- College Guidance Network admission video series: https://www.college
guidancenetwork.com/college-guidance-center-cgn

- Race to Nowhere: http://www.racetonowhere.com/

- Simon Sinek's Ted Talk: https://www.ted.com/talks/simon_sinek_how
_great_leaders_inspire_action

- The Social Dilemma: https://www.thesocialdilemma.com/

- Stephen Pyon's Ted Talk: https://www.ted.com/talks/stephen_pyon_what
_i_learned_through_college_applications

- *The TEST and the ART of Thinking*: https://www.thetestdoc.org/

- Thursday Night Live: Straight Talk with College Admission Leaders:
https://discover.derryfield.org/video-categories/thursday-night-live/

LISTEN UP

Podcasts

- Bucknell University's *College Admission Insider*
- Collegewise's *Get Wise: College Admissions Explained*
- Dartmouth College's *The Search*
- Ethan Sawyer's *The College Essay Guy*

- *Gangster Capitalism*, season 1
- GA Tech's *The College Admission Brief*
- *Have You Heard*, Episode #106, "School Rankings, Ratings, and Wrongdoing"
- National Association for College Admission Counseling's *College Admission Decoded*
- Scoir, Inc., *Inside College Admissions*
- *Your College-Bound Kid*

EXPLORE

College Search Tools

https://bigfuture.collegeboard.org/college-search

https://www.collegedata.com/cs/search/college/college_search_tmpl.jhtml

https://www.collegeraptor.com/

http://www.collegeview.com/collegesearch/index.jsp?crit=14

https://www.princetonreview.com/college-search

https://www.unigo.com/

https://www.scoir.com/

Virtual College Tours

CampusTours: https://www.campustours.com/

E Campus Tours http://www.ecampustours.com/

YouVisit: https://www.youvisit.com/

Standardized Testing

ACT: https://www.act.org/content/act/en/products-and-services/the-act.html

ACT Academy test prep: https://academy.act.org/

Fair Test: www.fairtest.org

Khan Academy SAT test prep: https://www.khanacademy.org/sat

SAT: https://collegereadiness.collegeboard.org/sat

Financial Aid and Scholarships

Department of Education: https://studentaid.ed.gov/sa/

Fast Web: www.fastweb.com

FinAid: www.finaid.org

Financial Aid Glossaries: https://studentaid.ed.gov/sa/glossary *and* https:// www.fastweb.com/financial-aid/articles/financial-aid-glossary

Going Merry: www.goingmerry.com

NACAC Financial Aid Resources: https://www.nacacnet.org/knowledge -center/financing-college/

NextStudent: www.nextstudentloans.com

RaiseMe: www.raise.me

Personal Finance Analyst Scholarships: http://www.personalfinanceanalyst .com/find-scholarships/

Sallie Mae: www.salliemae.com/scholarships

Scholarshiphelp.org: www.scholarshiphelp.org

Scholarships.com: www.scholarships.com

Studentawardsearch.com: www.studentawardsearch.com/scholarships.htm

Tuition Fit: https://www.tuitionfit.org/

Wired Scholars: www.wiredscholar.com

General

ACT: http://www.act.org/

Campus Safety / Crime Stats: https://ope.ed.gov/campussafety/#/

Coalition Application: http://www.coalitionforcollegeaccess.org/

College Board: http://www.collegeboard.com

Colleges That Change Lives: http://www.ctcl.com

Common Application: http://www.commonapp.org/

Education Conservancy: http://www.educationconservancy.org/

NACAC: http://www.nacacnet.org

NCAA: http://www.ncaa.org/

More Books on College Admission